WHISPERING THE LYRICS

Sermons For Lent And Easter Cycle A, Gospel Texts

THOMAS G. LONG

CSS Publishing Company, Inc.
Lima, Ohio

Copyright © 1995 by
CSS Publishing Company, Inc.
Lima, Ohio

Scripture quotations are from the *New Revised Standard Version of the Bible,* copyright 1989, by the Division of Christian Education of the National Council of the Churches of Christ in the USA. Used by permission.

Library of Congress Cataloging-in-Publication Data

Long, Thomas G., 1946-
  Whispering the lyrics : sermons for Lent and Easter : Cycle A, Gospel texts / Thomas G. Long
       p.   cm.
  Includes bibliographical references
  ISBN 0-7880-0492-1
  1. Lenten sermons. 2. Eastertide—Sermons. 3. Sermons, English. 4. Bible. N.T. Gospels—Sermons. I. Title.
BV4277.L66   1995
252'.62—dc20   95-14054
                                                                         CIP

This book is available in the following formats, listed by ISBN:
0-7880-0492-1 Book
0-7880-0493-X IBM 3 1/2 computer disk
0-7880-0494-8 IBM 3 1/2 book and disk package
0-7880-0495-6 Macintosh computer disk
0-7880-0496-4 Macintosh book and disk package
0-7880-0497-2 IBM 5 1/4 computer disk
0-7880-0498-0 IBM 5 1/4 book and disk package

.

PRINTED IN U.S.A.

With gratitude to Robert Morgan,
who demonstrates in all that he does
that teaching is a holy calling,
that people really matter,
and that grace is a way of life.

Editor's Note Regarding The Lectionary

During the past two decades there has been an attempt to move in the direction of a uniform lectionary among various Protestant denominations.

•Lectionary Uniformity

Preaching on the same scripture lessons every Sunday is a step in the right direction of uniting Christians of many faiths. If we are reading the same scriptures together we may also begin to accomplish other achievements. Our efforts will be strengthened through our unity.

•Christian Unity

Beginning with Advent 1995 The Evangelical Lutheran Church in America will drop its own lectionary schedule and adopt the Revised Common Lectionary.

•ELCA Adopts Revised Common Lectionary

We at CSS Publishing Company heartily embrace this change. We recognize, however, that there will be a transitional period during which some churches may continue for a time to use the traditional Lutheran lectionary. In order to accommodate these clergy and churches who may still be referring to the Lutheran lectionary we will for a period of time continue to provide sermons and illustrations based on scriptural passages from BOTH the Lutheran and The Revised Common lectionaries.

•For Those In Transition

Table Of Contents

C — Revised Common Lectionary; L — Lutheran Lectionary; RC — Roman Catholic Lectionary

Foreword

The Welsh tell a tale of an old preacher who was climbing the stairs into the pulpit one Sunday, as he had done on so many Sabbaths before, when abruptly he stopped halfway up, as if he had suddenly seen a ghost or become aware of some dreadful secret. He drew back down the stairs, his face filled with fear, and pointing with apprehension toward the pulpit, he cried to his startled congregation, "I will not . . . I will *not* go into that awful place."

Those who must preach during Lent and Easter recognize the old man's awe and dread. The road to Easter takes us through the most sacred stretch of the gospel story, and the narratives simply overwhelm us. Edmund A. Steimle, who for many years was professor of preaching at Union Theological Seminary in New York, once observed that the best image for a gospel sermon was not a package neatly wrapped and tied with a bow, but rather the rings left on the surface of a lake when a swimmer went down in deep water. The seasons of Lent and Easter, as every alert preacher knows, send us out into the deepest of the deep, and halfway up the pulpit stairs, we cannot decide whether it would be better to take the plunge and sink to the bottom or to back away and flee to the safety of the bathhouse.

Congregations who blithely assume that their pastors eagerly relish the chance to preach the passion and resurrection of Jesus are, for the most part, mistaken. To be sure, the pews are more crowded as Easter approaches, the choirs are well-rehearsed and in full voice, and an electric charge courses through the sanctuary, but the preacher stands there with the obligation to proclaim the truths of Jesus' death and resurrection, and it seems, at one and the same time, to be a set of claims too little to go on in a secular and cynical age and a range of mysteries too profound to speak.

So, let us admit it here at the beginning. These sermons, like all other sermons, must be found wanting. They are a stammered, confused, and finally pale and inadequate pointing toward the risen Christ. In some of them, the preacher, in a playful mood, leaps off the high dive and, mindless of the danger below, tries to turn somersaults on the way down. In most of them, the preacher, peering into the murky and churning depths, has to be pushed off the dive. In all of them, the preacher lands in water way over his head, and all that can be seen are the rings slowly spreading out from the place where he went down.

What happened to the old Welsh preacher? When he reached the bottom step, his sense of calling finally overcame his sense of dread. Taking a deep breath, he headed back up the stairs to the pulpit, opened his mouth, and preached. May God grant the same courage to all of us who must travel the road with Jesus to the cross and the empty tomb.

Thomas G. Long
Princeton, New Jersey

Two-and-a-Half Cheers For Hypocrites

It is difficult to find anyone who has a kind word to say about hypocrites. Nobody likes a hypocrite; no one wants to be around one; the last thing one would want to be called is a hypocrite. Hypocrites are, by definition, deceptive, two-faced and treacherous. If discovered, hypocritical politicians are defeated at the polls, hypocritical friends get dropped and hypocritical preachers lose the trusting ears of their congregations.

It may well be that our age is particularly tough on hypocrisy. In some ways, it is our one remaining public sin. We can tolerate embezzlement, infidelity, brawling and addiction in our public figures, but not pretense and hypocrisy. Presidential press conferences are scrutinized not only for major policy shifts but also for flickers of insincerity passing across the President's face, for the subtle twitch of an eyelid that would reveal the hypocritical dissembling beneath the high-blown rhetoric of statesmanship.

Several years ago, when a well-known television evangelist was caught *flagrante delicto* in a seedy, day-rate motel, it was not so much the deed itself that brought him low but the fact that his moral posturing, his wrenching, tear-stained appeals

9

for understanding and forgiveness, did not ring true in our ears. In short, he committed the unpardonable sin, the sin against the human spirit, the sin of trying to pull an emotional fast one — the sin of hypocrisy. "Father, do not forgive him, for he knows full well what he's doing."

Positioned on the scale of evildoing somewhere between tobacco company executives and junk bond traders, hypocrites are convenient villains for our cultural rage. In a therapeutic climate, where people clamor to appear on *Oprah* and *Geraldo* to do an emotional striptease, baring in the name of candor the deepest secrets of their past in front of an audience of perfect strangers, hypocrites seem, by contrast, emotionally stunted. They are guarded and deceptive; they put on false and pretty faces, hiding their true selves behind the cloak of pseudo-respectability.

Indeed, "hypocrite" was originally a theatrical term, describing actors, who concealed their real countenances behind dramatic masks. The sin of hypocrisy, then, is wearing a mask, and in our time no transgression is more contemptible. Hypocrites conceal sadness with a smile; they say they are happy to see you when they would rather have root canal work than to be in your presence; they give money to charities they do not truly support; they make speeches for causes they don't care about; and they laugh at jokes they don't find funny. In short, hypocrites wear masks, pretending to be who they are not.

Religious hypocrites are, of course, the worst of the breed — and the most inviting targets. In *The Devil's Dictionary*, Ambrose Bierce joined a long line of those who have skewered churchly hypocrisy when he defined a Christian as "one who follows the teachings of Christ insofar as they are not inconsistent with a life of sin" and a member of the clergy as one "who undertakes the management of our spiritual affairs as a method of bettering his temporal ones."[1]

The specific problem with religious hypocrites is that they are not only "holier-than-thou"; they are also "holier-than-themselves." They feign devotion, but it is mostly counterfeit.

.

10

As virtually every Youth Sunday sermon is quick to observe, hypocrites sit piously in pews (or stand piously in pulpits) on Sunday mornings praying the prayers and singing the hymns when, truth be known, they are really just as sinful as the secular types who have partied like jackals on Saturday and whose Sabbath liturgy consists of sleeping late and pondering what sort of toppings should go on the Domino's pizza they will order for the halftime of the football game. In fact, people with a sharp eye for hypocrisy would consider those who stay at home on Sunday as actually morally superior to the hypocrites who drag themselves out of bed and show up for Sunday school. At least they aren't wearing a pious mask and living a lie.

If we want to be hard on hypocrites — especially religious hypocrites — we seem to have a natural ally in Jesus. Whenever he got a card-carrying hypocrite in his sights, he pulled the rhetorical trigger. With rollicking humor, Jesus mocked hypocrites as the clowns of their own moral vaudeville show. As Jesus described them, hypocrites want the trumpeter to play "Hey Look Me Over" when they pull out their offering envelopes; they conduct prayer meetings at busy intersections during rush hour; and on fast days they put on a melancholy public face that makes them look for all the world like they have the flu. In short, they parade their deeds with a flourish before the admiring eyes of others. That's what they want, and that's what they get — indeed, the problem is that the adoration of the crowd is *all* they get. "Truly I tell you," Jesus says, "they have received their reward."

So Jesus does not tolerate hypocrites, and neither do we. So much for hypocrisy. Next topic . . .

But before we assume that Jesus fully shares our views on hypocrites, we should look again, and more closely, at what he says. To be sure, the hypocrites that Jesus takes on are people who are somehow missing the boat in their religious life, in their almsgiving, prayer and fasting, but that is not to say that there is nothing to them. Indeed, it must be acknowledged that they *are* people who give their money to the poor, who

11

pray and who fast. When he takes off after hypocrites, Jesus is not talking about people who thumb their noses at the synagogue or the church, and he is not talking even about those who show up for worship but sit passively on their hands. To the contrary, Jesus is talking about people every faith community desperately needs, people who actually put the faith into practice. They are people of charity, people of prayer, people of action. They are numbered among those who fill out their pledge cards, volunteer to keep the nursery, serve on committees, spearhead the social action task force and show up for church retreats.

In sum, in order to qualify in Jesus' book as a hypocrite one has to be what every church wants and needs — an active member, indeed an energetic *leader*. Hypocrites may have doubts and questions about what they teach in church school, but they teach. Hypocrites may demand brass plaques to mark their contributions, but they do give. Hypocrites may use flowery, sweetly pious language when they pray for the sick and the lonely, but they pray. Hypocrites may let it loudly be known that they volunteer a day a week to Habitat for Humanity, but they do build houses for the homeless. Two-and-a-half cheers for hypocrites; not quite three cheers, but applause nonetheless.

Indeed, Jesus does not attack religious hypocrites because they are so ruthlessly opposed to the gospel truth but rather because they have just barely missed it. Jesus says harsh things about the hypocrites not because they are so far away from the kingdom but because they are so very close and yet cannot see the true destination. The praying, fasting, almsgiving hypocrites of Jesus' day were not headed in the wrong direction; they were on the right path, but they did not take their faith far enough. They go only part of the way; they are willing to settle for the minimum wage of human adulation when so very near — just around the bend, in fact — lies the real treasure we all seek: the affirmation and intimacy of God.

Hypocrites are like some children who are behavior problems in school. Having lost the hope of being loved and cared for at home, they become show-offs in the classroom, creating spectacles of themselves for the amusement of others. Having despaired of the parental blessing, they settle for the momentary reward of the schoolroom spotlight. It is not the kind of attention they really need, but it is the attention they are sure they can get. Just so, hypocrites have lost sight of the blessing of the divine parent they have at home, lost sight of the God who sees in secret, who cherishes in the divine heart, who graciously rewards beyond measure. Therefore, they are condemned to parade around in front of the only audience they have left to impress — other people.

Jesus' harsh reprimand of hypocrisy, then, is intended to reclaim, not to destroy. Indeed, Jesus' scolding words are but white caps on a sea of providence. Underneath the reproach is the promise that God desires to draw near in mercy and redemption.

There is an old Hasidic tale about three pious Jews who decided to travel to a distant city to spend the high holy days with a famous rabbi. They set out on their journey, without food or money, intending to walk the entire way.

Several days into the journey, weak from hunger and still a long way from their destination, they knew they had made a mistake and they must do something. They came up with a plan. They decided that one of them would disguise himself as a rabbi. That way, when they came to the next village, the people would offer them food, honored to have a rabbi visit their town. None of the three, being pious, wished to be the deceitful one, so they drew straws, and the unlucky one who drew the short straw had to don the clothing of a rabbi. Another dressed as his assistant.

When they drew near to the next village, they were greeted with excited cries of joy, "A rebbe is coming! A rebbe is coming!" Escorted with great ceremony to the local inn, the hungry threesome were treated to a sumptuous meal.

When the meal was done, however, the innkeeper approached the "rabbi" and spoke with great sorrow. "Rebbe, you must pray for my son," he said. "He is dying and the

13

doctors have given up hope. But the Holy One, blessed be his name, may respond to your prayers."

The counterfeit rabbi looked desperately to his friends for help. They motioned for him to go with the innkeeper to his son's bedside. They had begun this hypocritical ruse, and now there was no choice but to keep on playing the game. The mock rabbi accompanied the distraught father to his son's sick bed.

That night, the three travelers slept fitfully. They were eager to leave town before their deception was discovered. In the morning, the innkeeper, still hoping for a miracle and grateful for the prayer of this visiting "rabbi," sent the party off with the loan of a carriage and a team of horses.

They left the village and traveled to the great city where they spent magnificent holy days under the spell of the famous rabbi. His teaching of the Torah carried their spirits to the very vault of heaven. But too soon, the holy days were at an end, and the three companions had to go back home through the same village to return the borrowed carriage and horses.

Terrified, the mock rabbi resumed his disguise; his heart was in his throat as they approached the village, especially when he saw the innkeeper running toward them, waving his arms furiously. But to the pretender's delight and surprise, the innkeeper embraced him with joy, exclaiming, "Thank you, rebbe. Only one hour after you left our village, my son arose from his bed well and strong. The doctors are amazed, but my son lives, and I am grateful for your faithful prayer."

The two companions looked with astonishment at their phony "rabbi" companion. What had happened? Had his prayer healed the boy? Was he truly a rabbi all along, without telling them? When they were alone, they turned on him with their questions. "What had he done at that boy's death bed?" they demanded to know.

He replied that he had stood at the boy's side in silence and, then, began to lift his thoughts to heaven: "Master of the universe, please; this father and son should not be punished just because they think I'm a rabbi. What am I? I am nothing! A pretender! If this child dies, his father will think a rabbi can do nothing. So, Master of the universe, not because of me, but because of this father and his faith, can it hurt that his son would be healed?"[2]

The Hasadim tell this story because of its profound insight into all of us. We are all pretenders, hypocrites. None of us is so worthy as to merit God's favor; our religion is a mask we hide behind. But God is gracious and redemptive in spite of our pretense.

Perhaps, then, Jesus reprimands the hypocrites because only a sharply pointed rebuke can poke a hole in the hypocrite's facade, allowing just enough light of the gospel to stream through with the news that every human being longs to hear: that when the applause of the admiring crowd dies out and the theater stands dark and empty and the pretender in all of us removes the mask and stands there, like the false rabbi in the old tale, all alone, there is still God — the God who knows our conduct grades and is well aware that we have primped around the classroom showing off for others, the God who nevertheless sees in secret, the God who looks behind the mask to find the child yearning to come home, and the God who beckons us to come just as we are.

---

1. Ambrose Bierce, *The Devil's Dictionary* (New York: Dover Publications, 1993), pp. 16-17.

2. This tale, from Jerome Mintz, *Legends Of The Hasadim* (University of Chicago Press, 1968) is retold by Belden C. Lane in his article, "Inadvertent Ministry," *The Christian Century* (November 7, 1984), pp. 1030-1031.

Facing Up To Temptation

Searching the aisles of the hardware store the other day for a tube of "Super Glue," I couldn't find it, so I went up to the customer service desk to ask for help from the young man standing at the cash register. He was on the telephone and, when he saw me coming his direction, he turned his back toward me. I could tell he was making a personal call, but I just waited. The call went on and on . . . "So did you like the movie . . . really? . . . Oh you're kidding! . . . What did Susan say? . . ." Finally I cleared my throat. He gave a sharp glance in my direction and kept on talking. "That Susan's fresh . . . Oh, I know, I hate that . . . So, you going to the game Friday? . . ."

I was now beginning to be impatient: "Pardon me," I said, "I need to ask one question."

He let out a great sigh and mumbled into the phone, "Catch ya' later, Charlie, I gotta go." He looked at me with an exasperated expression that said, "Well, spit it out."

"I'm looking for 'Super Glue.' "

"It's *on* the third aisle, in plain view," he said with disdain. As I walked down the third aisle, the farther I went the angrier I got. How dare he treat me, a customer, so rudely?

I was tempted to go back up there and give him a piece of my mind!

I was *tempted* ... what does that mean?

Talking to our friend Gloria the other day, she said that Frank (that's her husband) has all the luck. Seems that Frank has scheduled a mid-winter business trip to the Virgin Islands. "I could go with him," Gloria said. "He's got enough frequent flyer miles to take me along, and it surely would be nice to have a few days away from the cold and the routine. But our kids have school, and we'd have to leave them at home by themselves. With all the parties we've been hearing about when parents are out of town ... well, we trust them, but I hesitate to place them under that kind of temptation."

I hesitate to place them under that kind of *temptation* ... what does that mean?

The fellow next to me on the plane some time back was reading *USA Today*. "Well, there she is," he said, pushing the paper under my nose, making sure I saw the color photo of the attractive young woman in a bikini.

"Who is that?" I asked.

"Who is *that*? That's Kathy Ireland ... you know ... the cover girl for *Sports Illustrated*'s swimsuit issue."

"You going to buy a copy?"

He chuckled lecherously. "I dunno. I'm tempted."

I'm *tempted* ... what does that mean?

Most of us think that if there is one thing we know about in life, it's temptation. If there's one theological word that does not need to be rescued from abstraction, that connects firmly and vividly to our everyday experience, "temptation" would be the one. We face temptation all the time. Temptation hangs in our environment like flu virus, always threatening to break down our resistance. We are tempted to break our diets, flirt with somebody at work, finesse the chemistry test, cheat on our taxes, gossip about a friend, lie on our way out of trouble ... you name it. We are always being tempted to do what we know we shouldn't do. We don't need any instruction about temptation. Temptation we know about.

But, do we really? Do we really know what temptation is? Today's lesson from the Gospel of Matthew is a story about the nature of human temptation — Jesus' temptation and ours — and it throws a surprising light on what temptation really is.

What does it mean, really, to be *tempted*?

Several years ago, one of the books on the best-seller lists was the cleverly titled *All I Really Need To Know I Learned In Kindergarten*. In that book, author Robert Fulghum says that the deepest wisdom he knows about life was learned not at the top of graduate-school mountain but in the kindergarten classroom and in the sandbox playing with other children. Wisdom like: Share everything; play fair; clean up your own mess; say you're sorry when you hurt somebody; don't hit people; when you go out into the world, watch out for traffic, hold hands and stick together.[1]

Well, if Robert Fulghum got his deepest wisdom about ordinary life in kindergarten, perhaps the best place to search for wisdom about the life of faith, about a theological concept like temptation, can be found in Sunday school. Maybe all we really need to know about temptation we learned in Sunday school. Trying to remember what we learned in Sunday school may, however, be a stretch.

Frankly, I can't remember very much, but one pertinent comment did come back. Our church school teacher told us one Sunday, "The best measure of a person is what you would do if you knew no one would ever find out." Recalling that remark now, it strikes me more like general worldly wisdom than Christian wisdom, perhaps, but it's a near miss. It gets close to Christian wisdom, because our teacher was telling us that, when you take away all the lust for reward and all the fear of punishment — no one will ever find out — what you do in life grows out of who you understand yourself to be. In other words, our Sunday school teacher was moving toward a profound gospel insight: Christian ethics grow out of Christian identity; the decisions we make in life are a product of who we understand ourselves to be.

19

In that light, we have a far too shallow view of temptation. In ordinary terms, we think of temptation as the urge to do something we really would like to do but know we shouldn't do — one more cigarette, one more fling, one more drink, one more juicy rumor. But the deepest temptation is not the urge to misbehave, to do what we know we shouldn't do, but rather the enticement to compromise our baptismal identity, to be who we are not called to be.

That's the message in this story of Jesus' temptation. The devil is not tempting Jesus to misbehave. He is not tempting Jesus to steal a wallet, or sneak a peek at a *Playboy* centerfold, or cheat on his taxes, or pick a fight with his neighbor. It's deeper than that. The devil is tempting Jesus to ignore his baptism, to deny who he is, to forget that he is the child of his Father in heaven.

It is significant that Jesus comes to the temptation immediately from his baptism, when the skies opened and a voice from heaven said, "You are my beloved Son, the one with whom I am well pleased." That's who he is. "You are my beloved Son. You are the heir to the identity and mission of my people. You are my prophet, my priest, my anointed, my suffering servant. You are the one I am sending down the long and painful road to Jerusalem. You are the one I am calling to drink the bitter cup of sacrifice. You are the one I am delivering into the hands of those who will kill you. You are the one I am sending to bear the cross for the salvation of all people. You are the one to whom I am entrusting the promise of redemption. You are the one. You are my beloved Son, and I am well-pleased with you."

It is, then, when Jesus' vocation and identity are most clear that he comes to the season of his tempting. It is precisely Jesus' identity that the devil seeks to destroy. That, after all, is what temptation is all about. Notice how the tempter begins, "If you are the Son of God ..." He could have attacked directly: "You are *not* the Son of God," but he was too crafty for that. Much better to generate self-doubt — "*If* you are the Son of God" — since self-doubt is the cancer that eats away at identity.

20

Once, when my daughter was a teenager, we had one of those stormy father-daughter arguments. It blew over quickly, resolving itself in tenderness and understanding. But at the height of the squall I said, "Now you listen to me! If you're my daughter you ...." If you are my daughter? *If* you are my daughter? Flesh of my flesh, heart of my heart, my cherished and beloved daughter. I could hardly have used words more destructive than to raise doubts about her identity.

The devil picks away, then, at Jesus' sonship, at his baptismal identity. The three temptations — to turn stones into bread, to throw himself down from the top of the temple and to worship the tempter — are not enticements to *do* bad things; they are, at root, invitations to *be* somebody else, to live some life other than that of the beloved son of God.

Everything about the early chapters of Matthew — from the genealogy that opens the Gospel to the account of Jesus' baptism — makes it plain that Jesus had been given a narrative to follow, a storied identity, the narrative of God's salvation. The devil wants him to change the script, to trade God's story for some other story. Notice that Jesus combats the devil's attack not with theological innovation, skillful counter-arguments, or clever repartee, but by citing the story, quoting each time scriptures from Deuteronomy that he was taught as a child. In other words, Jesus resists the devil's wiles by quoting the holy script. He will not change the script; he will not live a narrative other than the one he has been given; he remembers his baptism, and he knows who he is.

Because we belong to Jesus Christ, we, too, have been given a part in the story, a role to play in this holy drama of redemption. We have been called, called in our baptism to be God's beloved children. In a world where might makes right, we have been named ambassadors of reconciliation. It is our baptismal identity to be those who sow love where there is hatred, hope where there is despair, faith where there is doubt.

Because we are called, we are also tempted, tempted to change the script, tempted to live out another story, tempted to be someone other than who we are called to be. To yield

21

to temptation is far more serious than to commit some transgression; to yield to temptation is to say, "I am not a child of God, and I will not take my part in God's drama of redemption."

In the midst of South Africa's struggle against *apartheid,* one of the most respected voices for racial harmony and human dignity has been that of Bishop Desmond Tutu. But even the closest colleagues of Tutu are sometimes distressed by the bishop's tolerance and moderation. They wish he would be more aggressive with his opponents. One of them said, "At his age you'd think he would have learned to hate a little more. But there is this problem with Tutu: he believes literally in the gospel." What he was saying, in effect, is that Tutu knows who he is, remembers his baptism. He knows the gospel story, and he will not change the script.

My senior year in high school I had a small part in the senior play. Truthfully, it wasn't actually a part *in* the play — I was far too shy for that — it was a part off-stage. I was the sound effects person. When the script called for knocking at the door, I rapped two sticks together. When the phone was supposed to ring, I touched the wires together on the battery operated bell, watching carefully so that I would stop just as the actor picked up the receiver.

We worked hard on that play. The director was a young woman who taught English at the school, a new addition to the faculty, and she poured herself into us and into the play. In the afternoons when school was out, she carefully coached all the actors on their lines and helped them get their timing right. She would then dash to get some fast food, returning to the school in the evenings for rehearsals. Afterwards, she would often stay late at night, working with us on the props and pitching in on the painting of the sets. Unselfishly she gave herself to this moment in our lives.

Night after night we rehearsed, and on opening night, we were ready; we had the play down perfectly. The curtains opened; the house was packed with our families and friends; electricity was in the air.

The first act was a dream. The play was a comedy, and every funny line evoked rich laughter from the audience. They were enjoying themselves, and we were, too. But in the second act, an actor forgot his lines. You could see on his face that he knew it was his turn to speak, but he could not find the words. The audience did not sense it yet, but the other actors and those of us off-stage did.

What to do? Everybody was paralyzed as this unfortunate classmate squirmed and tried to remember what he was supposed to say. I was standing in the wings, next to the young teacher who was the director. She was leaning toward the stage, every ounce of energy aimed encouragingly toward the struggling kid on stage.

The script in her hand, she was just about to whisper his line out to him, when suddenly he spoke. It was not the line in the script — in his anxiety, he just made something up — but he spoke. Not only that, what he said happened to be funny, and the audience roared with laughter.

Everybody on stage relaxed; they had gotten past a bad spot and could now work past it. Unfortunately, though, the forgetful actor heard the laughter of the audience and liked it, so he made up another line. This, too, was funny . . . not as funny as the first line, but the audience chuckled. So, the actor made up another line, and another, and still another.

The other actors were trying to respond to him, but they couldn't. He was out of control now, spinning off whatever came into his head. The play was disintegrating, lost. The audience had now figured it out, and what little laughter was left was nervous and mocking.

I don't remember how we got out of it, how we finished the play, or even if we did. The memory that sticks in my mind is looking up to see the director, the young woman who had given night after night of her time to work with us and make us ready, this woman who had poured herself into this play for our benefit, standing in the wings, watching and crying.

Jesus was cast into the lead role in the drama of God's redemption, and the devil tempted him to change the script, improvise on the character, deny who he was called to be. But Jesus knew who he was and he trusted his Father and he never changed the script. "It is written . . . It is written . . . God promised . . . ." Like Jesus, we who are part of the church have been baptized, and the words have been said about us, "You are a son of God . . . you are a daughter of God." We, too, have been given our parts to play in the drama of God's redemption. "Seek first the kingdom of God, pray without ceasing, repay no one evil for evil, feed my lambs, bear one another's burdens, be kind to one another, forgive one another, love your enemies, be merciful, even as your Father is merciful." Even now the tempter whispers in your ear, change the script, make up your own lines. Everything is at stake, and the one who has poured his life into preparing us is watching.

---

1. Robert Fulghum, *All I Really Need To Know I Learned In Kindergarten: Uncommon Thoughts On Common Things* (New York: Villard Books, 1988), pp. 6-7.

24

Too Soon, Monsieurs, Too Soon?

In the late 1950s, when "rock and roll" was still shocking and auto tail fins were the rage and television was laugh-tracking its way deep into the American psyche, no one had more fun spoofing popular music and art than Stan Freberg. An eccentric comic genius, Freberg left no cultural stone un-mocked. In dozens of song parodies and skits, he poked fun at icons, such as the flint-faced Sergeant Joe Friday of *Dragnet*, and at the more banal expressions of popular taste, such as Harry Belafonte's harmless West Indian ditty, "Day-O — The Banana Boat Song."

One of Freberg's better satirical sendups was an insipid French-language song on the American pop charts called "C'est Si Bon." The original recording featured a chorus of mellow-voiced baritones, who, at various points along the way, blandly chirped "si bon, si bon" in the background. In Freberg's parody, we hear the lead singer (Freberg affecting a very bad French accent) rehearsing his background chorus, "When eh gav' yew the sig-uh-nal, you will sahng 'si bon, si bon.' So wait, monsieurs, for the sig-uh-nal." But when the recording begins, the eager but tempo-impaired chorus will not wait for the signal; throughout the whole song, they jump the gun, always hilariously intoning their "si bon, si bon" a beat or a measure too early. "Too soon, monsieurs, too soon," the frustrated vocalist repeatedly cries in vain. "Please wait for the sig-uh-nal."

"Too soon, monsieurs, too soon." Many New Testament scholars have a similar reaction to the story of the transfiguration. With Jesus' face shining like the sun and his garments glistening like clothes in a television bleach commercial, the whole apocalyptically-flavored scene looks like a resurrection appearance that somehow broke loose from its moorings and drifted upstream to appear, prematurely, in the middle of the story of Jesus rather than at the end. This story of the transfiguration started its life as a resurrection narrative, these scholars say, and, therefore, it properly belongs at the *end* of the story — not here at the halfway point. So when Matthew, Mark and Luke insert this account in the middle of their narratives, some New Testament experts wag their fingers and chide, "Too soon, monsieurs, too soon."

Historically they may or may not be right, but theologically they are flat wrong. The transfiguration is not an ill-timed "Hallelujah Chorus" sung in error at intermission rather than as a finale. The transfiguration is strategically placed exactly where it ought to be: smack in the middle of Jesus' ministry. To be more specific, it is *the* midpoint, situated as a middle pier between Jesus' baptism at the beginning and his resurrection at the end, and one of its major purposes is to evoke the memory of the first and, at the same time, to whet the appetite for the second.

Indeed, according to Matthew's halftime report, Jesus' ministry is not faring well. The transfiguration occurs in a season of gloom. Jesus has been labeled a blasphemer, accused of demon possession, doubted by his friend and colleague in kingdom work John the Baptist, rejected by his hometown to the point that he stopped doing ministry there, resisted by the very people he came to serve and save, and is the subject of murder plots that will, of course, finally be successful.

26

In short, Jesus is plummeting rapidly toward the cross, and it is precisely at this moment of woe that he is transfigured. In a theological master stroke of timing, it is now — on this stretch of pathway through the valley of the shadow — that the transfiguration account calls us to remember Jesus' baptism and to anticipate his resurrection. As the storm clouds gather overhead, we hear from the skies the very same words we heard at the very beginning of his ministry, at his baptism, "This is my Son, the Beloved; with him I am well pleased" (Matthew 3:17). As the canvas of Jesus' life becomes fouled with the dark colors of death, here for a moment, he shines in splendor and unrivaled glory.

In other words, the placement of the account of the transfiguration is not a mistake in timing. It is a propitious and gripping promise of hope. Just when the mounting failure of Jesus' ministry threatens to cloud our vision with doubt — to provoke us to wonder, like John the Baptist, if Jesus is indeed the one we have been waiting for or whether we should look elsewhere to satisfy our deepest hopes (Matthew 11:3) — the curtains part for an instant, and we see who this Jesus truly is. "This is my Son," the heavenly voice reveals, "my beloved child, the one with whom I am well-pleased. He was my beloved Son at his baptism; he is still my beloved Son in the teeth of human rejection; and he will be my beloved Son in glory." As one creed puts it, "He was Lord at the beginning. He will be Lord at the end. Even now, Jesus is Lord."

In the main, then, the story of the transfiguration is a means of seeing — really *seeing* — who Jesus is right at the point that the deteriorating circumstances of his life and ministry threaten to obscure his identity. The transfiguration urges us not to be misled by the pain and the rejection of the present; this Jesus is, appearances to the contrary, the cherished Son of God.

But the transfiguration story is more. Because it is a way of seeing the truth about Jesus Christ, it is also a lens through which we may see the truth about ourselves and others. This story gives us what can be called the gift of "transfiguration discernment." Just as recognizing the true identity of Jesus required a parting of the curtain so that the blessing of the baptismal past and the glory of the resurrection future could shimmer through the gloom of the present, the same is true when Christians seek to understand themselves and others. To see who people really are requires more than a calculus of their present circumstances; we must view them with "transfiguration discernment," seeing them in the light of baptism and resurrection, the beginning and the end. As we muck it through in the mud and mire of the present, we are called to see people not only as they are but also as they were at the dawn of God's creation and as they will be in the triumph of God's future.

In order to become a minister in most denominations, a ministerial candidate must be examined and tested theologically. The church has a right and an obligation to know if a person is theologically sound before authorizing ordination, so theological questions are asked. I heard recently about a veteran minister who always asks the same theological question of every potential minister; indeed, he has been asking this question of every candidate for over 30 years.

He begins by asking the candidate to look out the window. The puzzled examinee peers out the window, and the old minister adds, "Tell me when you see a person out there."

"I see one," the candidate will haltingly announce.

"Do you know that person personally?"

"No, sir."

"Good. Now, my question is this: Will you please describe that person theologically?"

In three decades of experience in asking that question, the seasoned minister has found that the candidates tend to give one of two different answers. Some will say something like, "That person is a sinner in need of the redemption of Jesus Christ." Others, however, will respond, "Whether they know it or not, that person is a child of God, loved and upheld by the grace of God in Jesus Christ."

"I suppose," this minister reflects, "that, technically, both of these answers are theologically correct. But it is my experience that those who give the second answer make the better ministers." The reason, of course, is that they have the gift of "transfiguration discernment." They are able to see people in the present tense, in the middle of their circumstances, but they are able to see more than just the present tense. They can also see them as they were at the beginning of creation and as they will be in God's future — a beloved child of God.

When she called her minister to come to the hospital, she had just received the worst possible news from her physician. The cancer had returned with a vengeance, and there was nothing more that could be done. Her time was now a matter of weeks — or days. When her minister arrived, she shared the sad news and made her request, "I want you and some of the elders of the church to come here and, like the Book of James says, to pray for me and to anoint my head with oil."

The minister, a Presbyterian and unaccustomed to the ritual of unction, was startled by this request. "I'm not sure I can do this," he hesitated. "It seems more like magic than ministry."

She gripped his hand, "No. I am going to die. I *know* I am going to die. The doctors have made that clear. I am never going to leave this hospital alive."

"Then why do you want me to anoint you with oil?"

"Because it will be a sign that death is not the last word about me, a sign that I belong to Christ, a sign that in the power of God I am already healed."

So, around her bedside gathered her minister and a few others from the church. Long ago, when she was an infant, another minister had prayed over her, laid his hand upon her head and said the ancient words, "I baptize you in the name of the Father, and of the Son and of the Holy Ghost." Now, prayer was offered for her anew, hands were laid on her head again and the sign of the Holy Spirit was traced in oil upon her forehead. Here in the depths of her pain was a moment of transfiguration discernment. She — and everyone else in the room — remembered her baptism and glimpsed, even in the midst of her suffering, the glory of her resurrection.

Words, Words, Words

One doesn't have to search very far in our culture to realize that we live in an age that doesn't trust words very much. We use words by the bushel, in fact we are the age that does "word processing." Even so, we don't trust words; we build scaffolding out of them, but we don't put our weight on it. We know that words can be slippery, weasel things, used to conceal, to deceive, to distort. Words are cheap; people can hide behind words.

When a politician gives a speech, what do we say? Promises, promises. When the appliance repair shop says, "We'll be there to fix your refrigerator tomorrow at 2:00. You can count on it." We don't. When a president speaks boldly of building a "new world order" or assures us "I'll never lie to you" or coos soothingly "I feel your pain," we raise a skeptical eyebrow.

Rhetoric, talk, words — we don't trust them. Words are sneaky; talk is cheap. We don't want words; we want *substance*. As Eliza Doolittle says to her two suitors in *My Fair Lady:*

> *Words, words, words ... is that all you
>   blighters can do?
> Don't talk of stars burning above;
>   If you're in love,* show *me!*

31

Or, as Edgar Guest put it, uncomfortably closer to home: "I'd rather see a sermon than hear one any day ...."[1]

This distrust of words is nothing new, of course. Indeed, it's been there almost from the very beginning. According to the story of Adam and Eve, the situation began to deteriorate in Eden precisely at the point that the serpent began to raise the possibility that words just might not be all that they seem: "Did God say ...? Did God say you will die? No, those were just words; you will not die" (Genesis 3:1, 4).

At the dawn of creation, words were given as a gift from God. Animals make sounds, but human beings form words, potentially full of meaning and truth. Words were, in a sense, the first sacramental elements of communion. Whatever else we lost in Eden, we lost the trustworthiness of language. Men and women became afraid, and because they became afraid, they began to hide — from God and from each other — behind fig leaves and behind lying words:

"Where is your brother?"

"I don't know. Am I my brother's keeper?" (Genesis 4:9).

Now, all of this should give us some concern, since the things that we are called to do as Christians are done basically with words. Financiers have capital; physicians have medicines; farmers have seed and soil; soldiers have guns; Christians have words. Words, words, words. Prayer words, worship words, sermon words, words of hope, words of protest, words of praise. Where there is grief, words of comfort. Where there is injustice, prophetic words. Where there is complacency, challenging words. Words, words, words.

That is why it is important to hear the claim of the gospel that in Jesus Christ we get our words back, that the words we speak can become filled once again with grace and truth, can be renewed as instruments of redemption. That is part of what this story of Jesus and the woman at the well is all about. What did Jesus really do for this woman? He did not heal her of any disease; he did not raise her child from the dead; he did not dazzle her by turning the water into wine. He simply talked to her. Talked — that's all. Words, words, words. But the words he spoke were so radically different from the other words she had heard, words so filled with grace and truth, that she was never the same again.

It is important to note that this story does not begin with words. Quite to the contrary, it begins in silence. Not gentle, tranquil silence, but hard, cold silence. Because she who came to the well was a Samaritan; he who rested at the well was a Jew. She who came to the well was a woman; he who rested at the well was a man. Between Samaritan woman and Jewish man there was a wall of silence, built brick by brick with prejudice and hatred, through which no word was allowed to pass.

"Would you give me a drink of water?" said the Jewish man to the Samaritan woman, and the wall came tumbling down. One word, one seemingly ordinary phrase, a quiet word that cut against the grain of the culture, and the wall came tumbling down.

It is amazing how very significant moments of the church's ministry and the work of grace take place in not very dramatic ways. Sometimes, of course, there is the sensational confrontation with Caesar or the thrilling turnaround of faith, but most of the time, ministry is something like the quiet speaking of a single word. Like the December day in 1955 when a bus driver in Montgomery, Alabama, ordered four people in a row of seats to move to the back of the bus. It is said that one of these people, a department store clerk named Rosa Parks, spoke so softly that it was hard to hear her voice over the noise of the bus.[2] What she said was, "No," and a wall came tumbling down.

A minister tells about a young woman who was a member of a congregation he served. After college, she had entered pharmacy school, but from time to time she came home and worshipped with her parents. One Sunday evening, after one of her visits, the minister received a telephone call from her father. The father, somewhat upset, reported that his daughter had just called with the news that she had suddenly decided to drop out of pharmacy school. When the minister asked what could possibly have precipitated a decision, the father confessed that he had no idea and asked the minister to call his daughter and to "talk some sense into her."

When the minister did call the young woman, he expressed shock that she would decide to forfeit all of her hard work and that she should think long and hard before throwing it away. "How in the world did you come to this decision?" he asked her.

"It was your sermon yesterday that started me thinking," she replied. She went on to describe the theme of the sermon, that God calls everyone to a ministry, that God has some service for every Christian to do. She said that she realized that she was in pharmacy school for selfish reasons, to enter a lucrative career rather than to serve God. She had remembered a wonderful summer spent working as a part of a church program teaching reading to the children of migrant workers and how much she had felt that she was truly serving God then. So, after hearing the sermon that morning, she had decided to dedicate her life to working with underprivileged children.

There was a long silence on the minister's end of the line. "Now look," he finally said, "I was just preaching."[3] Words, words, words. Sermon words, words of the call of God . . . and the wall came tumbling down.

When the wall fell down between Jesus and the woman, she seems startled — perhaps even frightened. There's something comforting about a wall. It may hem us in, but at least we don't have to face what's on the other side of it. So, in shocked disbelief that the wall has fallen, perhaps even trying to rebuild the wall as a hiding place, the woman fires a flurry of words at Jesus. But beneath the words, Jesus hears the person; in the windstorm of her words, Jesus hears the woman:

> *"Why is it that you, a Jew, ask for water from a Samaritan woman?"* she asks.
> *"If you knew the gift of God,"* he replies, *"you could have asked, and he would have given living water."*

"Who do you think you are? You haven't even got a bucket. Even Jacob had to have a bucket. Are you greater than Jacob?"

Hearing her need, Jesus makes an offer. "Every one who drinks of this water will thirst again, but those who drink of the water I give will never be thirsty."

It was then that the woman said the fatal word, the word that caused the death of her old self, and gave her new life:

"Give me this water that I may never be thirsty," she pleads.
"All right," said Jesus. "Go call your husband."
"I have no husband."
"That's right. You have no husband. You've had five husbands, and the one you are with now is not your husband. You told the truth when you said you have no husband."

Now the commentators have raised their eyebrows about this woman, as if she were some sort of merry divorcee, the Liz Taylor of ancient Samaria, trading in husbands like sports cars. But all of their moral umbrage misses the point that women in the first century simply did not have that option. She has not devoured husband after husband; she has been devoured by a social system that, for whatever reason, has passed her from man to man to man until she no longer has even the dignity of marriage. Jesus is not so much exposing her sin as he is naming her subjection. With a word he has touched *the* issue in her life.

A former student of mine graduated from seminary and became the pastor of a small church, small enough so that she set for herself the goal of visiting every family on the roll in the first six months. At the end of six months, she had almost done it. She has visited every family, but one. "They haven't been here in two years," people said. "Don't bother; they aren't coming back."

35

She had set her goal, though, and so one afternoon she drove out to their house. Only the wife was at home; she poured cups of coffee and they sat at the kitchen table and chatted. They talked about this; they talked about that; then they talked about *it*. Two-and-a-half years earlier she had been at home with their young son. She was vacuuming in the back bedroom, had not checked on him in a while, so she snapped off the vacuum, went into the den and did not find him. She followed his trail, across the den, through the patio door, across the patio, to the swimming pool, where she found him. "At the funeral, our friends at the church were very kind. They told us it was God's will."

The minister put her cup down on the table. Should she touch it, or should she not? She touched it. "Your friends meant well, I am sure, but they were wrong."

"What do you mean?" she asked.

"I mean that God does not will the death of children."

The woman's face reddened, and her jaw set. "Then whom do you blame? I guess you blame *me*."

"No, I don't blame you. I don't want to blame God, either."

"Then how do you explain it?" she said, her anger rising.

"I don't know. I can't explain it. I don't understand why such things happen, either. I only know that God's heart broke when yours did."

The woman had her arms crossed, and it was clear that this conversation was over. The minister left the house kicking herself: "Why didn't I leave it alone?" A few days later the phone rang; it was she. "We don't know where this is going, but would you come out and talk with my husband and me? We have assumed that God was angry at us; maybe it's the other way around."

With a word, to touch the issues in people's lives. When Jesus named the issue in her life, the woman tried to change the subject:

> *"I see that you are a prophet," she said. "Now let's see, you prophets like to talk theology. Isn't it interesting*

*that you Jews worship in Jerusalem, and we Samaritans
worship on the mountain. Isn't that a fascinating theological difference. Would you care to comment on it? After you do, maybe we can move on to eschatology."
"Woman, I tell you," said Jesus. "The hour is coming, and now is, when the mountain, the temple, it won't
make any difference. What will make a difference is you
— your worship in spirit and in truth."
"Me? Make a difference? To God? When hell freezes
over . . . when Messiah comes."*

That's when Jesus said the best word of all. "I am he."
The one who, with a word, breaks down the walls. The one
who, with a word touches the deepest wounds of your life.
"I am he." In the beginning was the word . . . and the Word
became flesh and dwelt among us, full of grace and truth. "I
am he." Jesus was the Word, and because she was transformed
by that Word, she, who had been locked in silence, left that
place with a word to live and a word to speak. "Come and
see a man who told me everything I have ever done! Could
he be the Messiah?"

My uncle Ed ran an American Oil service station in a small
town in South Carolina. He was a wonderful man. He hunt-
ed and fished and told loud, uproarious jokes and people loved
him. While he was still a young man, his big heart failed him,
and the family gathered for the funeral. I was a young teenager
at the time. The minister at Ed's church was on vacation, and
despite assurances from the family that he needn't come back
for the service, he insisted and interrupted his time away to
return.

He drove half the night and all the next morning, arriving
just in time to come by the family home and to accompany
us to the church for the funeral. I will never forget his arrival.
Indeed, as I look back on it now, it created in me one of the
first stirrings toward ministry. The family was all together in
the living room of Ed's home, and through the big picture
window we saw the minister arrive. He got out of his stripped
down Ford, all spindle-legged, wearing a cheap blue suit,

clutching his service book like a life preserver. Now that I am a minister myself, I think I know what was going through his mind as he approached the house: "What to say? Dear God, what to say? What words do you speak when words seem hardly enough?"

What he did not know, could not know, is how the atmosphere in that living room changed the moment we saw him step out of his car. It was anticipation, but more than that. His arrival was, in its own way, a call to worship. This frail human being, striding across the lawn in his off-the-rack preacher suit, desperately trying to find some words of meaning to speak, brought with him, by the grace of God, the presence of Christ. In his presence and in his words — words, words, words — was the living Word.

And because the Word became flesh and dwells among us, so will it be for us, too. When we suck up our fear and venture out in faith into the tempest of confusion and hurt and try to find something — anything — gracious to say to people in need, the promise is that, by the mercy of God, our frail words become the earthen vessels for the Word so desperately needed, the Word that is Christ. So will it be for all of us.

---

1. Edgar A. Guest, "Sermons We See" as cited in John Bartlett, *Familiar Quotations,* fourteenth edition, edited by Emily Morison Beck (Boston and Toronto: Little, Brown and Co., 1968), p. 963.

2. Taylor Branch, *Parting The Waters: America In The King Years 1954-63* (New York: Simon and Schuster, 1988), p. 129.

3. Several versions of this story have appeared in sermons. The current one is adapted from William H. Willimon, *What's Right With The Church* (San Francisco: Harper and Row, 1985), pp. 112-113.

Lent 4 (C, RC)
Lent 3 (L)
John 9:1-41 (C, RC)
John 9:13-17, 34-39 (L)

Loving Jesus, Hating The Church

Those who analyze cultural trends have known for a long time that Americans seem to like religion a lot more than they like church. Whenever pollsters, pencils sharpened and questionnaires ready, knock on the doors of private citizens to inquire about their religious attitudes, it is difficult to find anybody out there who does not claim to be a fervent believer. If people are to be taken at their word, virtually everyone in the general population has a passionate and abiding faith in God.

Ironically, though, it is also increasingly difficult to find many out there who express this passionate and abiding faith in God by regularly showing up for worship at God's house. There is evidently a huge volume of passionate and abiding faith sleeping in on Sunday mornings. In America, as one wag put it, "People would be equally shocked to hear the faith doubted or to see it practiced."

Recently, a team of sociologists surveyed a representative group of several hundred "Baby Boomers" who had been raised in a serious and committed church environment. In fact, every person in the sample group had been confirmed in the church as an adolescent. When the research team tracked these people, it found that they still consider themselves "religious" — over 90 percent of these young adults describe themselves that way — but they do not bother much to express that religiosity in church — less than half of them regularly attend worship.[1] And, not unexpectedly, those who were not raised in a religious environment participate in church even less actively than the sample group, but that doesn't mean they aren't "religious," too; indeed, they are nearly unanimous in their willingness to affirm their devout belief. As the novelist Kingsley Amis wryly describes one of his characters, "He was of the faith chiefly in the sense that the church he currently did not attend was Catholic."[2]

Clearly, part of the reason why people are so quick to claim religious faith but not so ready to occupy a regular pew is that the church today no longer serves as the social crossroads of the community. In a pre-television land of villages and small towns, the church was not only a worship center but also a community center, a place where neighbors gathered, news was shared, stories swapped, recipes traded, rumors started and dispelled, romances begun and confirmed, great quantities of food consumed and newcomers welcomed into the community. People showed up at church because it was the place — in some ways, the *only* place — to be.

Recalling some of his growing up experiences, Jewish author Harry Golden wrote of his puzzlement, as a teenager, over his father's very active attendance at synagogue. Golden's father was a vigorous and outspoken rationalist and agnostic, yet he rarely missed a service. One day, Harry mustered enough courage to confront his father about this discrepancy. "Why do you go to synagogue," he challenged, "when you say you don't believe in God?"

Harry's father explained that there are many reasons why a person would go to synagogue. "Take my friend Dudja Silverberg," he said. "Dudja goes to synagogue to talk to God. Me? I go to synagogue to talk to Dudja."[3]

Going to the place of worship "to talk to Dudja" is a familiar and wonderful American tradition. Indeed, in the

40

Sabbath-go-to-meeting culture of previous generations, people would sometimes show up at the synagogue or the church house as much to meet and greet each other as to sing and pray. But now, fern bars, shopping malls, ski clubs, singles groups and on-line computer bulletin boards have replaced all that.

But this isn't the only reason that people stay away from church. Sure, there are other, more convenient places for social interaction, and television and rented videos easily outstrip the entertainment value of most worship services. But the fact is that a good many people do not participate in church because they flatly do not like the organized church. The problem is not distraction or indifference; it's repulsion.

Many in our culture are simply repelled by the whole idea of the church as an institution. Pick any given Sunday morning and approach the guy teeing off at the golf club, the woman pruning the shrubs, the couple prowling the local shopping plaza, the sports fan tuning in *The NFL Today*, the family spreading out a picnic at the lake, the numberless legion sleeping in until noon, and ask virtually any one of them, "Do you believe in God?" The reply, almost surely, will be, "Oh, yes, most certainly." But when we add, "Then, why are you not in church today?" the predictable reply is, "Actually, I haven't been since I was a kid. You don't have to be in church to worship God" or, more bluntly, "Frankly, I'm not into organized religion."

At the very least, such thoughts reflect the underlying assumption that the church, with its institutional trappings — its clergy, stewardship drives, potluck suppers, roof repairs, educational programs and bureaucratic entanglements — is simply a heavy, unnecessary and optional shell around true faith. Vibrant faith needs no institutional husk; it flutters free of its churchly cocoon and soars through the air unencumbered, alighting as easily on the ninth fairway as it does on the communion rail.

More intensely, such attitudes view the church as worse than a mere indifferent shell; they see the church as the enemy of authentic faith. Religious institutions, some say, actually squelch genuine belief. Faith is full of grace, but the church is too often saturated with law. Faith dances; the church tends to wag its finger. Faith is freedom; the church is bound up with rules and regulations. Faith is the inner child; the church plays the angry parent. Faith is flexible; the church is rigid. Faith invites; the church indicts. Faith sees you as a person and wants you to be fulfilled; the church sees you as a "giving unit" and wants you to fill out a pledge card. Faith wants you to think for yourself; the church demands mindless conformity to a fixed creed.

"Tell the truth," demands one of the characters in Alice Walker's *The Color Purple*, "have you ever found God in church? I never did. I just found a bunch of folks hoping for him to show. Any God I ever felt in church I brought in with me."[4]

Those holding this view of religious institutions as the enemy of living and personal faith can certainly find some potent ammunition in the biblical story about the man who was blind from birth. In a dramatic moment of grace, he was healed by Jesus. But almost as soon as this happened, as soon as this man experienced one of the most transforming spiritual moments possible, he was hauled before the religious court, subpoenaed by the officials of the holy system to account for himself.

The problem, strictly speaking, was not that the man was healed of his blindness — everybody knew *that* was a good thing — but it was the fact that Jesus happened to heal him on a sabbath day — which was considered a bad thing since it violated the accepted organizational interpretation of the sabbath commandment. The result was a deadly combination for rigid religious institutions — a good thing that doesn't fit the rules.

Quite naturally, it divided the house. Some of the leadership pounced on the bad part, declaring Jesus to be way out of bounds: "This man is not from God, for he does not observe the sabbath" (John 9:16). Others, however, pondered the good part, and wondered whether instead of waving the rule book they ought to waive it in the light of this great paradox, mainly that a man who appears to fit the description of "sinner" nonetheless performs such wonderful, gracious and holy signs, like healing this blind man (John 9:15).

The rule keepers won the argument, of course — they usually do — and, to demonstrate that they held the power and were still in control, they intimidated the family of the newly healed man (John 9:22) and, finally, unceremoniously bounced him right out the front door of God's house (John 9:34). It mattered not that this was his hometown, his neighborhood congregation, his place of worship since he was a child; his unconventional religious experience rendered him *persona non grata,* and out he went.

We seem to have, then, a textbook case of the repressive religious institution at work. As long as people are "blind," the welcome mat is out, but let them start to see a little light, let them begin to think for themselves, let them start tapping their feet to the Spirit's tune instead of the official march, and the religious police move in with handcuffs and billy clubs.

The man has been healed of his lifelong curse, for goodness' sake, but all the institution is concerned about is whether it fits the Book of Discipline. The man had a momentous, life-changing religious experience, but all the officials can do is debate whether it conforms to the creed. The man can see — at last he can *see* — but all the religious system wants to discover is whether it was properly scheduled on the church calendar. This is typical of the institutional mindset, and who could blame this man if he chose to spend the rest of his sabbaths sleeping late, playing tennis all afternoon and muttering, "Frankly, I'm not into organized religion"?

Thus, the theme of this story seems to be Jesus versus the institution. Jesus saves; the system spanks. So, love Jesus and seek out a life-giving personal relationship with him, but keep your distance from all "organized religion" and don't take any creed classes or fill out any pledge cards. As one television evangelist is quick to say, "We need a lot more Christianity and a lot less 'Churchianity.' "

There is a serious problem, however, with this view. The problem is Jesus. Jesus will not cooperate with any neat schemes that pit true Christian experience against doctrine and church. To be sure, the religious leaders are eager to force their theological straitjacket on the healed man. They want to make sure that Jesus hasn't colored with his crayons outside the accepted doctrinal lines. Even so, when Jesus comes to the man after he has been tossed out of the institution, astoundingly, the first thing he does is to give him a theology lesson and the next thing he does is to talk about the community of faith (the sheep of the fold — John 10).

Jesus does not say to the man, "Now that you have your eyesight you can finally get free from all that moldy doctrine and that repressive religious organization." No, Jesus teaches the man theology — the key theological concept of the "Son of Man" — and then teaches everybody about how the sheep belonging to God are gathered together — that is, are "organized" — into a community of believers who trust and obey the voice of the Good Shepherd.

The thrust of our story, then, is not spirit versus institution, not living experience with Christ versus dead creeds, not loving Jesus and hating the church. What this story calls us to do is to think about the kind of church we ought to be, the sort of institution and organization the Christian community should seek, the style of leadership and theology we ought to nurture.

When we think about it this way, the key to the story jumps out in the form of a curious statement of Jesus. The religious leaders, haughty and defensive, challenge Jesus, "Surely we are not blind, are we?" Jesus responds, "If you were blind you would not have sin. But now that you say, 'We see,' your sin remains" (John 9:41).

The sin of the leaders, then, is that they think they see, that they think they perceive the truth with crystal clarity, that they think they have grasped with their minds the depth and breadth of God. The true community of faith, on the other hand, seeks to know God, but holds its knowledge in humble hands. It is always ready to admit that everything it sees it sees through a glass darkly and that God may at any time break our idea of the rules and do something outside the lines, like healing a man on the wrong day of the week or raising a man from the tomb who was supposed to stay dead. The church stays light on its feet, thankful for what it knows and expects, but ever ready to pray, with the old preacher, "O God, let something happen this morning that isn't in the bulletin."

A friend who had been raised on a family farm in South Carolina and who had always lived on this ancestral land became engaged to marry a woman whose family had moved many times in her childhood. My friend, for whom the land meant stability and permanence, asked his once fiancee, "If you moved so many times, what is home to you?"

She thought for a moment and then replied, "The furniture."

He knew what she meant. No matter how many moves they made, how many towns they lived in, the furniture was always there. Perhaps there is a parable here for the church. Because God is always surprising us, always breaking the rules and performing wonders we did not plan, the faithful community must be ever ready to move. Its structures and programs are not the land; they are the furniture. Its creeds and rules of procedure aren't a stone fortress; they are tent pegs.

In the mid-1970s, priest Henri Nouwen spent seven months in a Trappist monastery near Rochester, New York. As he participated in the patterns of this very organized religious institution — the liturgy, the silence, the regulated rhythms of the day and week — he gradually understood that, at its best, the structure was not for itself but, rather, to "create space for God." He wrote in his journal, "The monk, more than anyone else, realizes that God dwells only where [we step] back to give him room."[5] He went on to say,

> *Monks go to a monastery to find God. But monks who live in a monastery as if they had found God are not real monks. . . . God should be sought, but we cannot find God. We can only be found by him . . . .*[6]

Indeed, we cannot find God; we can only *be* found. And that, in the end, is what this story of the blind man is all about. John tells us that Jesus "found him" (John 9:35), and despite our brave talk about searching for the honest truth, the honest truth is that what we most yearn for in our souls is to be found by him, found by the Good Shepherd who lays down his life for the sheep.

So, we sit in the pews and open our hymnals to sing God's praise; we stand to recite the creed and we join the inquirer's class to learn something about what we are saying; we support the programs of the church and even fill out a pledge card. We do these things not because we think we have the truth of God all figured out; we do these things because these are the ways God's people "create space for God." We do these things because we trust and hope that we, too, will hear the words, "You have seen [the Son of Man], and the one speaking with you is he" (John 9:37).

---

1. Donald A. Luidens, Dean R. Hoge, and Benton Johnson, "The Emergence of Lay Liberalism Among Baby Boomers," *Theology Today,* Vol. 51, No. 2 (July, 1994), pp. 249-255.

2. Kingsley Amis, *One Fat Englishman,* as quoted in *The Oxford Dictionary Of Modern Quotations,* edited by Tony Augarde (Oxford and New York: Oxford University Press, 1991), p. 4.

3. Harry Golden, *The Right Time: An Autobiography* (New York: G. P. Putnam's Sons, 1969), pp. 24-25.

4. Alice Walker, *The Color Purple* (New York: Harcourt, Brace, Jovanovich, 1982), p. 165.

5. Henri J. M. Nouwen, *The Genesee Diary: Report From A Trappist Monastery* (Garden City, New York: Doubleday, 1976), p. 148.

6. *Ibid.,* p. 118.

Bad Timing

Some people are masters of bad timing. These are the people who burst into a party wearing a lamp shade and a hula skirt just as the conversation has taken a serious turn, a turn, say, toward a discussion of human rights or world hunger. Masters of bad timing buy high and sell low. They are the folks who try to rouse the hayriding young people to one more chorus of "She'll Be Coming 'Round The Mountain" just as the mood has shifted to the romantic. They telephone with questions about corrections to the minutes of the Christian Education Committee during the fourth quarter of the Super Bowl. Once, some years ago, they traded in their Edsels for Studebakers. They cannot help themselves; they are masters of bad timing.

The mother of the sons of Zebedee — that is, the mother of James and John — is such a person. Taken in isolation, what she does in this story is perfectly understandable. If we cut her a bit of slack, it is perhaps even admirable. She is a mother looking out for her children. In context, however, this woman, like a blacksmithing major at the local vocational college, is a living embodiment of bad timing.

What she does, of course, is to act on her concern about the job potential of her two sons. No surprise there; parents have been anxious about their children's vocational advancement as long as there have been children heading out into the world. Moreover, with James and John, there was undoubtedly reason for apprehension. After appearing to have settled on the family fishing business, the two brothers had abruptly gone into the admittedly shaky field of discipleship (Matthew 4:21-22), and their mother is merely inquiring of their boss if the two had made a career mistake. How high can the boys reasonably expect to go up the ladder? "Would it be possible," she asks Jesus, "for them to be in top management when the kingdom comes? In fact, if it's not too much to ask, could one sit on your right hand and one of your left at the Board of Directors' table?"

There is nothing very pretty or very subtle about this mother's request, but there is also nothing very unusual about it either. Strong-willed parents are forever lobbying on behalf of their children; it happens all the time. Such a routine parental inquiry may well have gone unnoticed, forgotten along with the thousands of other stems and pieces of everyday conversation, noble and ignoble, that must surely have passed among Jesus and his followers as they toiled along the road to Jerusalem, except for its unmistakable and outrageous bad timing.

It is the eternal misfortune of Ms. Zebedee to have raised the question of her sons' exaltation while there was still ringing in the air Jesus' moving speech about his own coming humiliation. Her craving questions about ambition, prominence and glory land directly on top of Jesus' words about the suffering, disgrace and crucifixion that await him. Jesus has just announced to his disciples that the road he is travelling will take him directly into the heart of shame, where he will be mocked and flogged and crucified. The mother of James and John could hardly have picked a more inopportune moment to pump Jesus for information about her sons' employee benefits program — but such is the skill of a true master of bad timing.

But we should be fair to her. First of all, she has not been present to hear Jesus' speech. There is no way she could have known that her brassy bid for her sons to have the best seats at the kingdom power lunch would be spoken into the face of one of the gospel's most humble and sorrowful moments. Her bad timing — as is usually the case with bad timing — is simply a matter of poor luck (or, more likely, the overlapping of her story and Jesus' speech about suffering is a piece of literary irony created by the gospel writer for dramatic and theological effect).

Second, she and her sons are by no means the only ones concerned about positions of honor and power. The rest of the disciples may wish to paint on meek faces and pretend to be shocked and hurt by Ms. Zebedee's chutzpah. But the fact that the other disciples, when they hear what she said, became peppery and aggravated (Matthew 20:24) is a sign that they, too, have been wondering about those choice places to the left and right of Jesus. They are less offended by Ms. Zebedee's brass than by the fact that she has broken in line and beat them to the punch.

The point, then, is not to single out the mother of James and John for our amusement or our scorn. True, what she does is an atrocious, almost ludicrous, example of bad timing, but the purpose of the story is not to make a comic figure out of *her* but, rather, to see *ourselves* in her, to discern the sort of bad timing that threatens to undo us all.

Let us try, then, to see ourselves in her, to grasp how her drive typifies and represents what is in us, too. First, this mother's question expresses a fundamental human craving for recognition. We all want that, too. Behind even the most humble and self-sacrificial face there is a human being who covets stature and credit. Andy Warhol predicted a future in which every person would achieve the universal human quest to be famous, but only for 15 minutes. A nineteenth century lighthouse keeper at Cape Hatteras wrote this prayer in his log: "O Lord, do not let any ship wreck upon the sea this night. But if it be Thy will for such to happen Lord, I beg Thee, let it happen here.'' He did not wish for a ship in distress, but, if it were going to happen anyway, why shouldn't he be the rescuer whose name got in the newspaper?

Much of the society we have built for ourselves is aimed at the crasser forms of acquisitiveness and jockeying for position. When the Chicago Chamber of Commerce held a contest to create a new promotional slogan for the city, one local newspaper columnist wryly suggested that a genuinely representative motto would be "Where's Mine?'' The mother of James and John wants to know what all of the disciples want to know — what all of *us* want to know: What's in this for me? Where's mine?

The second step is to admit that her bad timing is really ours as well. Ms. Zebedee can perhaps be pardoned for making an untimely entrance into the gospel story because she had no idea there was a gospel story — but *we* do know the gospel story. To know the gospel and still to relish the spotlight, to lust for power and reward is a master stroke of bad timing.

Admittedly, in terms of drama, the mother of James and John chose one of the worst possible moments to press her case, but when do we think would have been a better time? Read through the pages of Matthew's gospel and see if you can find a more fortuitous moment for her to advance the cause of her sons. Perhaps she should have interrupted Jesus during the Sermon on the Mount just as he had proclaimed, "Blessed are the meek, for they will inherit the earth'' (Matthew 5:5). Or maybe she could have sidled up to Jesus with her power request just as he had warned a would-be follower, "Foxes have holes, and birds of the air have nests; but the Son of Man has nowhere to lay his head'' (Matthew 8:20). Or what about the occasion when Jesus was sending out the twelve with no money and no luggage to do kingdom work — to cure the sick, raise the dead, cleanse lepers and cast out demons? (Matthew 10:8-10).

The point, of course, is that there simply is no suitable time in the gospel for self-serving ambition. She is not merely a moment or two off time; she is an eon out of phase. What makes her request for prestige and rank inappropriate is not that she picked the wrong instant but that she picked the wrong age. In the life and ministry of Jesus the world has shifted on its axis and the seasons of humanity have changed. The whole business of greed and power plays and stepping all over people on the way to achieving one's "personal best" is now a piece of permanent, eternal, immutable bad timing because in Jesus "the kingdom of heaven has come near" (Matthew 4:17).

So, the message of the gospel is not *carpe diem*, but "repent"; not "watch for the right moment to make your move," but "follow me"; not "vertical advancement," but "whoever wishes to be great among you must be your servant" (Matthew 20:26). Everything that once was in season is now obsolete. We can throw away our old clocks; we can cast our outdated calendars in the trash bin. The kingdom age of mercy and righteousness and peace has arrived; everything that rivals it is bad timing.

Many years ago in India, a group of men travelling through desolate country found a seriously wounded man lying beside the road. They carried him to the Christian mission hospital some distance away and asked the missionary physician who met them at the door if a bed was available for the man. The physician looked at the injured man and immediately saw that he was an Afghan, a member of the warring Patau tribe. "Bring him in," he said. "For him we have a bed."

When the physician examined the man, he found that an attacker had seriously injured his eyes and the man's sight was imperiled. The man was desperate with fear and rage, pleading with the doctor to restore his sight so that he could find his attacker and extract retribution. "I want revenge," he screamed. "I want to kill him. After that I don't care whether I am blind the rest of my life!"

The doctor told the man that he was in a Christian hospital, that Jesus had come to show us how to love and forgive others, even to love and forgive our enemies. The man listened but was unmoved. He told the doctor that Jesus' words about forgiveness and love were nice, but meaningless. Revenge was the only goal, vengeance the only reality. The doctor rose from his bedside, saying that he needed to attend to other patients. He promised to return that evening to tell the man a story, a story about a person who took revenge.

When he returned that evening, the doctor began his story. Long ago, he recounted, the British government had sent a man to serve as envoy to Afghanistan, but as he traveled to his new post, he was attacked on the road by a hostile tribe, accused of espionage, and thrown into a shabby makeshift prison. There was only one other prisoner, and the men suffered through their ordeal together. They were poorly clothed, badly fed and mistreated cruelly by the guards.

Their only comfort was a copy of the *Book Of Common Prayer*, which had been given to the envoy as a farewell gift by his sister in England. She had inscribed her name along with a message of good will on the first leaf. This book served the men not only as a source for their prayers but also as a diary, as a place to record their daily experiences. The margins of the prayer book became a journal of their anguish and their faith.

The two prisoners were never heard from again. Their families and friends waited for news that never came; they simply vanished without a word, leaving those who loved them in uncertain grief.

Over 20 years later, a man browsing through a second-hand shop found the prayer book. How it got there, no one can say. But, after reading some of the journal entries in the margin, he recognized its value, located the sister whose name was in the front of the book, and sent it to her.

With deep heartache she read each entry. When she came to the last one, she noted that it was in a different handwriting. It said simply that the two prisoners had been taken from their cell, publicly flogged and then forced to dig their own graves before being executed.

At that moment she knew what she must do. Her brother had died a cruel death at the hand of torturers in a run-down Afghan jail, and this injustice must be requited. She must exact revenge . . . but Christian revenge.

She was not wealthy, the doctor continued, but she marshaled all the money she could and sent it to this mission hospital. Her instructions were that the money was to be used to keep a bed free at all times for a sick or wounded Afghan. This was to be her revenge for her brother's torture at the hands of Afghans and his death in their country.

The wounded man was quiet, silenced by this story of such strange revenge. "My friend," said the doctor, "you are now lying in that bed. Your care is her revenge."[1]

The sister knew the gospel, and because she knew the gospel she also knew that the time for vengeance was over. In Jesus Christ, revenge and hatred, which once seemed so urgent and timely, are now obsolete. The kingdom age of mercy and forgiveness and peace has arrived.

Anything else is simply bad timing.

---

1. *Peace Be With You,* edited by Cornelia Lehn (Newton, Kansas: Faith and Life Press, 1980), pp. 67-68.

When Jesus Arrives Late

It is very easy to move too quickly past the beginning of this story about Jesus and Lazarus. We rush past the beginning because the rest of the story appears, at first glance, to be far more fascinating. Indeed, most of the time it is what Jesus did all the way at the end of the story that galvanizes our attention. There, after all, is the main drama, since it was at the end of the story that Jesus performed his most astonishing miracle: raising Lazarus, deceased four days, from the dead. Jesus had done a number of other miracles in the Gospel of John, of course. He had turned water into wine, healed a paralyzed man and restored sight to a man blind from birth. But to raise someone from the dead? This was breathtaking, unheard of, a remarkable sign of the inbreaking of the eternal, an anticipation of Jesus' own resurrection. No wonder the end of the story attracts our gaze; it is where the fireworks are.

Sometimes, however, when we have finished our amazed gazing at the end of the Lazarus story, we still have enough energy to shift our sights to what Jesus did in the middle of the story — namely, he wept. This piece of the narrative is fascinating, too. "Jesus wept" (John 11:35) is the shortest verse in the Bible, at least in the King James Version, but it is not the easiest verse to understand. Why did Jesus weep? Is he moved with grief over the death of his friend Lazarus? Is he in sorrow over the unbelief around him? Is he anticipating his own death, too? John does not say.[1] But even though the reasons for his feelings remain somewhat mysterious, we are still drawn to this picture in the middle of the story of an emotionally affected Jesus, tears slowly falling down his cheeks.

Because Lazarus' raising at the end of this story is so dramatic and Jesus weeping in the middle so enigmatic, it is, therefore, easy to overlook the beginning of this story. What at the beginning could possibly rival the action in the middle and at the end? To do so, however, would be a loss, for there is something curious and important at work there as well.

What is most intriguing about the beginning of this story is the fact that Jesus is intentionally tardy, that he plans his schedule so as to arrive on the scene belatedly. Jesus receives word that Lazarus is ill in the village of Bethany, but John makes it clear that Jesus was in no hurry to respond. In fact, John draws attention to Jesus' delay. John says that *even though* Jesus loved Lazarus and his two sisters, Mary and Martha, nevertheless, Jesus waited two days after he heard the news to go to Bethany (John 11:5-6). By that time, of course, it is too late. Lazarus is dead.

Both Martha and Mary pour salt into the wound by pointing out to Jesus that his tardiness has cost a life. "Lord, if you had been here," they both say, "my brother would not have died" (John 11:21, 32). Indeed, Jesus was not there, intended not to be there, and Lazarus did die. John waves a flag over this fact so that we will not miss it.

Our temptation is to judge Jesus harshly here. What kind of person would dally around while a friend lies dying? What could possibly have kept Jesus where he was while Lazarus, whom he loved, sweated out his last few breaths on his death bed? What Jesus did seems to be a violation of basic human compassion not to mention a scorning of the elementary instincts of pastoral care. Why in heaven's name, we ask, was Jesus late?

And that, it turns out, is precisely the question the author of John wants us to ask. Why *in heaven's name* was Jesus late? John knows that if we keep asking that question, we will discover something profound about heaven's name, about Jesus and about God's ways in the world. But what? What good can we possibly find in Jesus' tardiness?

Part of what we will find is that Jesus sometimes saves us by being absent rather than present, at least not present in the ways we demand or expect. Later in the Gospel of John, Jesus tells his disciples that he will soon depart from them. "You will look for me," he says, ". . . [but] where I am going, you cannot come" (John 13:33). This announcement that Jesus plans to separate himself from the disciples causes fear, perhaps even panic, to set in. The disciples cannot imagine being apart from Jesus. They plead that they will be lost without him (John 14:5), beg to be allowed to follow him (John 13:37), but Jesus refuses. He clearly intends to be their Lord by being absent from them.

What this means is that Jesus will be obedient to God's will and not theirs. Jesus will accomplish the saving work of God and not their small and local understanding of who he should be. They want him to be the leader of their little band, but Jesus is the light of the whole world. They want him to teach them, guide them, heal them, protect them, save them; Jesus teaches, guides, heals, protects, and saves all humanity. They want him to respond to their immediate concerns, but his mission is not captive to their sense of what is urgent. He is their Lord because he transcends their little world; he is their Lord because he is Lord of all.

On Sunday morning, July 17, 1966, arguably the most newsworthy worship service in the world that day was held in St. Peter's Cathedral in Geneva. A great congregation had gathered, including Christian leaders from all over the globe. Reporters from around the world were present to cover this event. The service had been planned as a part of the World Council of Churches Conference on Church and Society, and there was an exceptional air of expectation that day since

57

the sermon for the morning was to be delivered by the world famous civil rights leader Dr. Martin Luther King, Jr.

But Dr. King did not show up for the service. The hymns were sung, the prayers were prayed, and the ecumenical affirmations were spoken, but the pulpit was empty that day. Dr. King was absent. He had canceled his trip to Geneva because racial rioting had erupted in the city of Chicago, and his presence was needed there as a mediator. He sent a video tape of an excellent sermon to Geneva, and it was played over television monitors at the appropriate time, but, as one of the worshippers pointed out, "Even more powerful than his sermon that day was the simple fact of the preacher's absence."

"Even more powerful . . . was the preacher's absence." In other words, Dr. King chose to be absent in a place where he was expected to be present because of his larger sense of mission. If he had been a politician looking for a photo opportunity, he would no doubt have shown up in the Geneva pulpit, smiling for the cameras, rather than risking his life and reputation amid the chaos of Chicago's violent streets. But given the wider scope of Dr. King's ministry, what appeared on the surface to be the most important place for him to be, St. Peter's Cathedral, was not, in fact, where his vocation took him.

In an even deeper sense, Jesus' mission transcends our tiny definitions of urgency. A man was dying. More than that, it was Jesus' friend Lazarus who was dying. Lazarus' body grew weak, hot with fever. Mary and Martha were wringing their hands with worry. The whole village of Bethany was troubled. Naturally, from Bethany's perspective, this was the most urgent, important, life or death crisis in all of creation, and Jesus should have dropped everything in the world to be there. But Jesus will not drop the world; he will save it, all of it. Jesus is not controlled by illness and death, even his dear friend Lazarus' illness and death; to the contrary, Jesus is the one in control. Jesus does not jump when illness and death say "jump," he conquers illness and death for the entire human race.

Not only will Jesus not allow illness and death to set his agenda, neither will Jesus allow death to be the ruler of time. In the world as we know it, death is in charge of time. When the hospital's intercom crackles with the message "Code Blue," a signal that a patient has suddenly gone into cardiac arrest, all normal time ceases. Physicians and nurses abruptly interrupt their customary duties and rush with emergency equipment to the afflicted patient. Routines are halted; all other activities must wait. Death has sounded the alarm and pushed the stem on the stop watch, and all must urgently obey death's timetable.

But not Jesus. He gets the "Code Blue" on Lazarus, receives the word that the old clockwatching slavedriver death has punched in "911" and his immediate presence is demanded. But Jesus does not respond to death's timetable. Jesus is Lord over death and Lord of all time. No longer will death set the times and seasons, but only God. So, Jesus takes his time, because it is, after all, *his* time. He is the Lord of the sabbath, and he is the Lord over Monday, and Thursday, and all the ticking minutes and desperate seasons of life. He is Lord over all time. He was there in the beginning, before all time, and through him all creation, including time, came into being.

There is a couple in Arkansas who have given their six-year-old son strict instructions to come home from playing every afternoon no later than 5 p.m. He is allowed to play with his friends, but his parents are quite serious about his curfew. If he is not home by 5 p.m., they begin to worry and call around the neighborhood to find out where he is. The boy knows this, though, and is careful to arrive every day on time.

One April Monday, however, the day after Daylight Saving Time went into effect, the boy was late coming home. When he finally arrived, a few minutes before 6 p.m., his mother scolded him for being late. "You know you are to be home by five," she said, "and here it is nearly six."

Puzzled, the little boy pointed out the window. "But the light," he protested, "the light; it's the light that tells me when to come home."

Realizing what had happened, his mother smiled and gently explained that the day before the time had been changed, that everyone had reset their clocks and, now, the daylight lasted longer.

The boy's eyes narrowed. "Does God know about this?" he asked suspiciously.

In a childlike way, this little boy shared John's theological vision. Time finally belongs not to human beings, not to the corruption of illness and death, but to God. We know what time it is not by death's clock, but by Jesus' light. Jesus arrived in Bethany on his schedule, not death's. When he got to the tomb of Lazarus, now dead four days, Jesus, the Lord of past, present, and future, reached into the future of his resurrection victory and reversed the past of Lazarus' death, thereby displaying the glory of God in the present.

"God so loved the world," John writes, "that he gave his only Son, so that everyone who believes in him" can change their clocks. Instead of watching the clock, wondering when death will finally come calling to stop the hour hand from moving, those who believe recognize that Jesus came calling with life eternal. When Jesus at last came calling on the little village of Bethany, it was the common verdict that he was woefully late. But when Lazarus danced away from the tomb of death, the light of eternal life in his eyes, the whole world could see that Jesus was right on time.

---

1. For a helpful discussion of the mystery of Jesus' weeping, see Fred Craddock, *John* (Atlanta: John Knox Press, 1982), pp. 87-88.

Passion/Palm Sunday
Matthew 26:14—27:66* (C, RC)
Matthew 26:1—27:66 (L)

What A Friend He Had In Judas

Tourists who travel to faraway places will often attempt to learn a few useful phrases in the language of the land where they are going. They will practice typical traveler's lingo like "My name is Sarah. What's your name?" or "I am from St. Louis in the United States" or "Waiter, would you please bring our check?" or "Excuse me. I'm lost . . . can you show me the way to the Hotel Pierre?" or "Thank you very much."

One of the real tests of knowing another language, however, is cursing. If we don't know what not to say, if we don't know the profanities and insults of another culture, we can easily embarrass ourselves. Being able to order in a restaurant or to rattle off a few pleasantries is, of course, helpful, but really getting inside a language and culture means being aware of the off-color as well as the colorful, the taboo words as well as the polite ones. It is unsettling to try to request a room at a hotel but, because we choose the wrong phrase, to end up inadvertently slandering the desk clerk's mother.

In a small college town in the South, they still tell the story of the international student in the early 1970s who learned

*Sermon emphasis Matthew 26:47-50

61

his idiomatic English by watching Archie and Edith Bunker on *All In The Family*. Not quite catching all the nuances, this student began wandering into the town shops, smiling a toothy grin, and greeting local merchants with a cheery, "Hello, dingbat!" If one does not really know another culture, it is easy to make such a mistake, to mean to offer a greeting but to end up slinging an insult.

The same thing is true, in a curious way, about the Gospel of Matthew. There are curses and insulting terms hidden in the grain of ordinary language. If you don't know your way around in Matthew, you can accidentally poke somebody with a sharp tongue.

Take the word *rabbi*, for example. "Rabbi" is a good and acceptable title. Some of the most respected and honored people in our society are called "rabbi," indeed prefer to be called this. Not in Matthew. In Matthew, *rabbi* is a taboo term. At one point, Jesus even specifically forbids his disciples to use it (Matthew 23:8). Many scholars believe that this was because Matthew's church, Jewish by heritage, was in the middle of a painful and unfortunate shouting match with the rest of the local Jewish community. Some think that this little Christian community, because of their divisive devotion to Jesus, had been dismissed unceremoniously from the synagogue. Whatever the case, the word *rabbi* had a sour taste in their mouths, and it was not a term to use in polite company.

For less obvious reasons, the word *friend* is also a verbal slap in the Gospel of Matthew. In the Gospel of John, *friend* is a good word. "What a friend we have in Jesus." Not in Matthew. When someone calls somebody else "friend" in Matthew, it has a kind of "Okay, Buster, back off" flavor. For example, in the parable of the Laborers in the Vineyard (Matthew 20:1-16), when the workers who have worked all day long begin to grumble about their wages, a provoked vineyard owner looks one of them straight in the eye and retorts, "*Friend*, I am doing you no wrong." Or again, in the parable of the Wedding Banquet (Matthew 22:1-14), when one of the guests is found stuffing himself with hors d'oeuvres and lurking around the punch bowl but not wearing the proper wedding attire, an offended host shames him with a verbal blast: *"Friend,* how did you get in here without a wedding robe?" If somebody calls you "friend" in Matthew's gospel, you've been called on the carpet.

Rabbi and *friend* — words of respect and endearment in most settings but insults in the local lingo of Matthew. How fascinating to find these two terms coming together in Matthew's description of the betrayal of Jesus by Judas.

What happens is this: The time of Jesus' death has come. He has shared a last meal with his disciples and then, separating himself from the others, prayed the great prayer of anguish in Gethsemane's garden. Rising from prayer, he returns to the disciples and announces ominously, "See, my betrayer is at hand."

Right on cue, Judas rattles on stage with a clumsy band of thugs armed with swords and clubs. Judas and his cohorts have a secret signal: Judas will go up to Jesus and kiss him. That way, Judas no doubt reasoned, the toughs will know which one is Jesus but the kiss will be a perfect camouflage. Jesus will be fooled into thinking that Judas is still a devoted and loving disciple.

It didn't work. If the armed hooligans were not enough of a giveaway, Judas betrayed himself with his own words: "Greetings, Rabbi!" he burbled as he smeared the kiss on Jesus' cheek. Greetings *rabbi*?

"Friend," replies Jesus, not missing a beat. *"Friend,* do what you are here to do." What Judas was there to do, of course, was betrayal. What a friend he had in Judas.

In Matthew's book, when Judas uses the term *rabbi*, he shows his true colors. In that seemingly innocent title is contained all of Judas' misunderstanding of Jesus, all of his treachery, all of his misguided collaboration with the enemy.

But when Jesus calls him "friend," it must be heard at two levels. There is, first, the bitterly ironic level. Standing there with hateful heart, his insincere kiss and his armed posse, Judas is no friend of Jesus. So, for Jesus to call him "friend" in this moment of treason is to use the word in Matthew's peculiar glossary, as a caustic barb, a verbal jab. "Well, what do we have here? If it isn't my good friend, my old pal, Judas." But because he is Jesus, there is another level, too. Because he is Jesus and because he was from the very beginning the one who would "save his people from their sins" (Matthew 1:21) and because he was the savior who called Judas, even Judas, to be one of his own, there is another level of meaning in his words. Jesus calls Judas "friend" because, at the deepest level of all, Jesus *is* his friend. At the deepest level of all, Jesus is the friend of Judas, and he is the friend of all the disciples who "deserted him and fled" (Matthew 26:56), and he is the friend of all of us . . . we who, like Judas, do not know how to love him and are betrayers of his trust.

The late Lewis Grizzard was a newspaper columnist and essayist known for his offbeat, often outrageous, Southern humor. Beneath the laughter, however, there was sadness — a life of personal suffering and loss. Some of Grizzard's pain came from his troubled relationship with his father, an alcoholic who left the family when Grizzard was a boy. "Before he died," he wrote, "I asked Daddy a thousand times, 'What is wrong? Why can't you stay sober? Why can't you stay in one place? What can be so bad you can't talk about it?' " His father would never give a direct answer.

One day, Grizzard pled desperately with his father to tell him what was wrong in his life. He told him that it didn't matter what it was, no matter how terrible, that he loved him whatever was the awful truth. But his father could not respond. He could only weep, sobbing out the words that he had made a mistake, "a bad mistake."

"That's all I ever got," said Grizzard. "The man died, so far as I know, with his secret. What terrible . . . secret did he have? Did he kill somebody? Did he rob or cheat somebody? Was he a child molester? . . . I can think of no more unthinkables. No matter. Whatever his sin, his secret, I loved him — and I love him — anyway."[1]

.

64

Whatever his sin, I loved him — and I love him — anyway. This is a moving tribute from a son to a wayward father. In a vastly more powerful way, it is a description of the gospel itself, of the unwavering love of Jesus Christ for all of us, all of us who, like Judas, have secrets too shameful to tell.

Matthew tells us that Judas repented. He went to the temple and confessed his sin to those who had hired him, but he found no forgiveness there. So, throwing down the 30 pieces of silver, Judas, tragic Judas, feeling as though he had not a friend in the world and unable to bear his sin, took his own life. But Judas did have a friend, a friend who loved him to the end, and even though Judas could not bear his own sin, his friend bore it for him on the cross.

In Arthur Miller's play *The Price,* two brothers, Victor and Walter, have come home after their father's death to divide the property. The relationship between the brothers, always strained, erupts into bitterness. Old wounds are freshly opened; words of spite are spoken; new hurt is produced. At the end of the play, the brothers part angrily. Reflecting on this broken and resentful relationship, Victor's wife Esther says,

> *So many times I thought — the one thing [Victor] wanted most was to talk to his brother, and that if they could — But he's come and he's gone. ... It always seems to me that one little step more and some crazy kind of forgiveness will come and lift up everyone. When do you stop being so ... foolish?*[2]

"One little step more and some crazy kind of forgiveness will come and lift up everyone." When Judas, the betrayer, had done his deed, Jesus took that one step more. He stepped of his own free will onto the cross of sacrifice. No one took Jesus' life; he gave it willingly. And when he did, "some crazy kind of forgiveness" lifted up the broken world, and all that destroys human life, all the hatred and the betrayal and the venom and the decay and the disease and death was absorbed and overcome in the eternal friendship of Jesus Christ.

1. Lewis Grizzard, *My Daddy Was A Pistol, And I'm A Son Of A Gun* (New York: Dell Publishers, 1988), pp. 108-110.

2. Arthur Miller, *The Price,* Act Two (New York: Viking Press, 1968), p. 113.

Maundy Thursday
John 13:1-17, 31b-35 (C)
John 13:1-17, 34 (L)
John 13:1-15 (RC)

Good News,
Bad News, Good News

I forget now whether it was a famous football coach, a former president, or a positive-thinking teacher who put on his wall the motto, "When the going gets tough, the tough get going" — probably all three of them. In any case, I am aware of the fact that there are some people who pride themselves on being able to get motivated in tough situations, to face head-on the tough issues. "Give it to me straight, Doc," they say to the surgeon, "I can handle it." They sign up for courses from the roughest professor on campus, not in spite of, but *because* she hasn't given an *A* since 1953. They aren't drafted by the Army; they volunteer for the Marines. No Novacaine for them at the dentist, no sir. Unlike many others, these folks don't whine; they don't grumble; they don't look for the easy way out. The tougher things get, the more they thrive.

So, when they arrive at a biblical text like ours today, the story about Jesus washing the disciples' feet, their approach is, "Okay, don't sugar coat it. What's the hard news in this good news?" They don't see any sense in being mollycoddled, so if there is a tough and demanding word from Jesus here, let's have it. "Give it to me straight, Doc, I can handle it."

Thus, they comb through the story, looking for the "baddest, toughest" thing there, and, sure enough, they find one. Jesus says, "So, if I, your Lord and Teacher, have washed your feet, you also ought to wash one another's feet."

There it is, the unvarnished "bad news" in the good news of this story — Jesus' demand for lowly, footwashing service. But the tough types do not flinch at this mandate. They want no euphemisms, no spiritualizing metaphors. They know that footwashing means exactly what it sounds like — humble, ignoble, service to needy people in the name of Christ. It will mean things like cleaning up the church soup kitchen, letting others take the glory for the successful church program even when you did the work, comforting people whose not-so-nice lives are coming apart, loving the unlovely, being ready to see the worst side of others and still be compassionate.

None of this will be easy, of course, but, the gospel isn't supposed to be easy. Dirty feet are dirty feet, but they still must be washed. That's Jesus' tough word, and when the going gets tough . . . .

The irony, however, is that the toughest word in the story is not this one. The toughest word in the story about Jesus' washing the disciples' feet is not that they will have to turn now and wash each other's soiled feet. As hard as that may be on occasion, they can do that. The genuinely toughest word in this story is that, first, before they do anything, the disciples will have to sit still and allow Jesus to wash *their* feet. Notice that the disciples do not balk when Jesus commands them to wash others' feet; the resistance comes — voiced by Peter — to *being* washed.

So, the hard message in this text is not that we will have to give; it is that, before we have anything to give, we must receive from Jesus. Jesus did not wash the feet of only one disciple; he washed the feet of all of them. He did not wash Peter's feet alone and then say, "All right, you have the idea. Now Peter, you do that to James, and James to John." No, each disciple was obliged to put his feet in the basin, to feel the water between his toes, to experience the hands of Jesus, his teacher and Lord, rubbing away the dirt and drying his ankles with a towel.

So, if we are searching for the unvarnished truth, the real "bad news" in this good news story, is this: "Unless I wash you, you have no share with me" (John 13:8). In other words, without receiving this ministry from Jesus, we cannot be a disciple. Lacking his grace, apart from his service, without his act of self-sacrifice, we have nothing, absolutely nothing to give. "Nothing in my hand I bring," goes the old hymn, "only to the cross I cling."

This is particularly "bad news" for the tough part of us, the self-reliant and resourceful part. The hardest word in this story is not that we have a demanding task of ministry to do, but, if we will only stiffen our resolve, we can do it; the hardest word is that we cannot do it, not on our own strength. As Dag Hammerskjold once said, "How frightful is our poverty when we try to give others something of ourselves."

There is a certain congregation that, for the past ten years, has taken a hunger offering on the last Sunday of every month. During the singing of the final hymn, members of the congregation stream down the aisles with their offerings and place them in baskets on the communion table. Half of the money goes to local hunger needs, the other half to global programs.

This is a fairly affluent congregation and one deeply committed to social causes, so the monthly hunger offerings are usually quite substantial. The congregation is rightfully proud of the amount of money they have raised over the years, the hunger programs they have helped finance and the difference their offerings have made.

One Sunday morning, however, as the final hymn was being sung and as people were making their way forward with their offerings, a stranger moved down the aisle toward the communion table. She was clothed in the unmistakable dress of one who has spent the night in the street. As she drew closer to the offering baskets, many in the congregation began to notice this homeless woman and watch her curiously. Was she planning to make a contribution? She, after all, was the kind of person this offering was for. Some confessed later that they suspected that she might attempt to take money from the baskets.

But when she got a few feet from the communion table, she paused and, in her own way, made an offering. She slowly folded her hands and began to pray silently. Prayer was the only offering she had to give, but it was the most fitting and generous offering made that day. This woman, in her poverty, taught a tough-minded and affluent congregation that ministry is not a matter of our strength, but God's. This needy woman reminded a confident and self-reliant flock that ministry is not a matter of economic power but of prayer. By her prayer, this unwashed woman revealed to a well-scrubbed congregation our common human need, that we all have dirty feet, and unless our Lord washes us clean we have nothing to offer.

The theologian Karl Barth once said of preachers that the only appropriate attitude for them to assume was embarrassment. Preachers should be embarrassed, said Barth, because they stand before congregations to give them what they do not, themselves, have — the Word of God. They are utterly dependent upon what they do not possess and cannot control, God's freely given grace; without that, they have nothing to say.

The same is true of all Christians. The church has no wisdom but God's, no mercy but Christ's, no insight but the Spirit's. Unless we stretch out our dirty feet toward the basin of Jesus' grace and allow ourselves to receive from him, we have no gifts to give.

Belden C. Lane, a university professor whose scholarship has focused on the study of narrative and storytelling, was invited some years ago to be one of the featured storytellers at a storytelling festival. Lane was both excited and frightened by this request. He had often taught classes on narrative and used stories in his teaching, but he had never been in the position of telling stories to a critical audience in a performance setting.

When he arrived at the festival, terrified, he crossed paths with another of the featured storytellers, a woman from New

70

York well-known for her skill. He shared with her how scared he was, saying, "I don't feel like a real storyteller."

"You know," she said, "I don't think there are any storytellers. There are only stories, and each of us gets to carry one of them for a little while."[1]

Just so, there are no real disciples in the self-sufficient sense; there are only people who are given the blessing of carrying the work and presence of Jesus Christ for a little while. Unless Jesus gives us the work, unless he grants us his presence, unless he washes our feet, we have nothing.

In this sense, the experience of having their feet washed by Jesus was, for the disciples, like the parable of the Good Samaritan for the cocky lawyer who asked Jesus, "And just who *is* my neighbor?" When Jesus, in response to this question, began to tell the tale, it was innocent enough, and the lawyer surely identified with the anonymous man traveling down that Jericho road. Everybody had made that trip; the lawyer himself had done so, and now he was traveling the road again in his imagination.

It is a dangerous journey, though, and, sure enough, the traveler — and, vicariously, the lawyer — got mugged and was discarded in a gutter, left for dead. In his imagination, the lawyer watches from the ditch as a priest and a Levite come along, but carefully cross the road so they can pass by without getting involved with him.

Finally a Samaritan comes, and like Peter when Jesus reached out to wash his feet, the lawyer surely recoiled. Who would want to be touched by a Samaritan? But the Samaritan stopped, dressed the injured man's wounds, took him to an inn, saw that he was cared for in his need.

"Who turned out to be the neighbor?" asked Jesus. In other words, "You, Mr. Lawyer, were in that ditch. How did it feel? Who proved to be a neighbor to you?"

The lawyer, his zeal for self-justification beginning to wilt, admits, "The one who showed him — the one who shows *me* — mercy."

Then — and only then — Jesus said, "Go and do likewise." The fact is, the lawyer could not possibly have gone and done likewise before he heard the parable. He would have had nowhere to go, nothing to do, nothing to give. It was only when, through the story, he had experienced neediness, experienced the destruction of his self-reliance, experienced the gracious touch of one whose help he would, in stronger moments, have disdained, that he had anything to go and do. He needed to receive grace before he could possibly give it to others. Until Jesus had washed his dirty feet, the self-assured lawyer had no ministry to perform.

Sociologist Robert Wuthnow of Princeton University has explored how it is that people make everyday ethical decisions. Many people, he found, perform deeds of compassion, service and mercy because at some point in their past someone acted with compassion toward them. "A narrative about care received becomes part of our autobiography," he writes. "The caring we receive may touch us so deeply that we feel especially gratified when we are able to pass it on to someone else."[2]

He tells the story of Jack Casey, who was employed as an emergency worker on an ambulance rescue squad. When Jack was a child, he had oral surgery. Five teeth were to be pulled under general anesthetic, and Jack was fearful. What he remembers most, though, was the operating room nurse who, sensing the boy's terror, said, "Don't worry, I'll be right here beside you no matter what happens." When Jack woke up after the surgery, she was true to her word, standing right there with him.

Nearly 20 years later, Jack's ambulance team is called to the scene of a highway accident. A truck has overturned, the driver is pinned in the cab and power tools are necessary to get him out. However, gasoline is dripping onto the driver's clothes, and one spark from the tools could have spelled disaster. The driver is terrified, crying out that he is scared of dying. So, Jack crawls into the cab next to him and says, "Look, don't worry, I'm right here with you; I'm not going anywhere." And Jack was true to his word; he stayed with the man until he was safely removed from the wreckage.

72

Later the truck driver told Jack, "You were an idiot; you know that the whole thing could have exploded, and we'd have both been burned up!" Jack told him that he felt that he just couldn't leave him.[3]

Many years before, Jack had been treated compassionately by the nurse, and because of that experience, he could now show that same compassion to another. Receiving grace enabled him to give grace. "Unless I wash you," Jesus said, "you have no share with me."

So, this story of good news has some "bad news." We are not able in our own strength and on our own resources to care for others, even those closest to us. But this "bad news" is really the best good news of all, for Jesus takes the basin and the towel and tenderly, mercifully washes our soiled feet and our tarnished souls.

1. Belden C. Lane, "Inadvertent Ministry," *The Christian Century,* (November 7, 1984), p. 1030.

2. Robert Wuthnow, "Stories to Live By," *Theology Today,* XLIX/3, pp. 308-309.

3. *Ibid.,* p. 308.

The Seven Last Words Of Pilate

Some stories in the Bible are so essentially visual that they almost demand that we act them out to understand them. Like the rest of the Bible, such stories are intended to be read and heard, of course, but they have the added quality of being vivid, pictorial, perhaps even theatrical, and they seem to release their full power only when they are seen in action. In order to grasp their truths, we are compelled to scramble up on a stage — at least one constructed in our imagination — to don a costume, to summon a cast of supporting actors, and to put the story into dramatic motion.

It is one thing, for example, to hear the story of Zacchaeus; it is quite another actually to see him — this tiny man swallowed by the always-taller crowd; this lilliputian tax collector lost in a sea of NBA centers; this diminutive bureaucrat flexing himself up on his tiptoes, craning his neck in vain as he tries to find a decent sight line, finally lifting his skirts and shinnying immodestly up the nearest sycamore tree. Or again, it is one thing to read Jesus' parable of the lost sheep, but quite another to experience it in the theater of the absurd. In the

*Sermon emphasis John 18:28—19:22

75

ear it all sounds rather manageable, perhaps even tame: A sheep is lost, the shepherd goes to find it, and that's that. But to the eye it releases its outrageous truth. To watch in astonishment as a seemingly sane shepherd walks away from 99 perfectly good sheep, leaving them to the perils of the wilderness, while he searches with wild and passionate abandon for one scraggly runaway is to be confronted with some extravagant and unruly grace at the heart of the gospel.

The story in the Gospel of John of the trial of Jesus before Pontius Pilate is another example of a biblical story that discloses itself only through dramatic reenactment, a story that must be seen in motion to be believed. Only when we allow the primary characters to move through their paces do we discern how intricate and intriguing a piece of theological drama we have here.

What becomes most evident in the staging of this story is the restless and ceaseless activity of Pontius Pilate, tramping in and out of his headquarters, pacing back and forth time and again. Such fretfulness is unexpected. He is, after all, the chief judge in this trial; he is the one ostensibly in charge. What we would expect of him is resolute calm, perhaps even bored passivity. We imagine him heavy-lidded and drowsy, interrogating Jesus between barely stifled yawns as he sleepwalks his way through yet another procedural matter. Or maybe we anticipate Pilate scarcely paying attention to Jesus' testimony, his mind's eye wandering lazily past this insignificant Galilean and out the open window to the beckoning freedom of the coming holiday weekend.

Whatever we expect, it is not the fitful, fidgety Pilate that we see when we put this narrative into production. Not just once, not just twice, not even three times, but seven times — *seven* times — Pilate changes location.[1] Out to the crowd he stamps, then back inside the headquarters to confront the prisoner, then returning to the shouting mob, only to rush back inside, and on it goes. We have, then, seven moves by Pilate, seven scenes, seven glimpses of a nervous and troubled politician, seven shifting moods, seven occasions for Pilate to speak his mind and to reveal his soul before he shuffles off the canvas of history into infamy — in sum, we find here the seven last words of Pilate.

But what does this seven-fold shuttling mean? What is disclosed as we track this turmoil and overhear the seven last words of Pilate? To begin with, we discover that the roles have been reversed. It is Jesus who is calm, Pilate who is frenzied. It is Jesus, the accused, who resolutely presides as judge; it is Pilate, the prosecutor, who acts out the inner conflicts of the defendant.

In the scenes out on the porch, as Pilate faces the restive crowd, every speech shows him more and more convinced of Jesus' innocence and more and more fearful of the political consequences. Inside the headquarters, every statement shows Pilate more and more confounded by this mysterious presence. Pilate is no poised diplomat; he is a ping-pong ball slapped back and forth between his public fears and his inner doubts. He pleads, he bullies, he begs, he vacillates, and finally he folds: "Then he handed Jesus over to them to be crucified" (John 19:16). The irony is clear: It is Jesus who is convicted, but it is Pilate who is guilty. It is Jesus who is to be crucified, but it is Pilate and all like him who are defeated. It is Jesus who will suffer death, but it is the world that is perishing.

During the prime days of the struggle for racial integration in the South, black civil rights workers — "freedom riders" they were called — would travel on buses from city to city, challenging segregationist laws. Sometimes they were greeted with violence; often they were arrested. In one town, a bus was halted by the police and the passengers booked and jailed. While they were there, the jailers did everything possible to make them miserable and to break their spirits. They tried to deprive them of sleep with noise and light during the nights. They intentionally oversalted their food to make it distasteful. They gradually took away their mattresses, one by one, hoping to create conflict over the remaining ones.

Eventually the strategies seemed to be taking hold. Morale in the jail cells was beginning to sag. One of the jailed leaders, looking around one day at his dispirited fellow prisoners, began softly to sing a spiritual. Slowly, others joined in until the whole group was singing at the top of their voices and the puzzled jailers felt the entire cellblock vibrating with the sounds of a joyful gospel song. When they went to see what was happening, the prisoners triumphantly pushed the remaining mattresses through the cell bars, saying, "You can take our mattresses, but you can't take our souls." It was the hymn singers who were in jail, but it was the jailers who were guilty. It was the prisoners who were suffering, but the jailers who were defeated. It was the prisoners who were in a position of weakness, but it was the broken and bigoted world of the jailers and of all the Pontius Pilates of history that was perishing.

But there is an even deeper truth to be found in the seven last words of Pilate. As we hear this thin and shrill voice crying out Jesus' innocence to the mob, as we hear his nervous questions — Are you a king? What have you done? What is truth? Where are you from? — it slowly dawns on us that we are listening to the unmistakable cadences of Christian worship. Everything Pilate says finds an echo in the church's liturgy. Pilate unwittingly assumes the role of congregational worship leader:

"Is he a king?" liturgist Pilate calls out.

"Yes," responds the church, "the kingdoms of this world have become the kingdoms of our Lord and his Christ, and he shall reign forever and ever."

"What is truth?" prompts Pilate.

"*He* is. He is the way, the truth and the life."

"Where is he from?" Pilate prods, continuing the litany.

"He is from God on high," sings the church in reply.

Most ironically moving of all is the moment when Pilate leads the congregation in a violent doxology. Repeatedly striking Jesus across the face, Pilate and his cohorts nonetheless bow down before him and unintentionally sing an Easter hymn: "Hail, King of the Jews!" (John 19:3).

.

78

The point of it is that, even in its starkest moment of violence, the world nevertheless glorifies Jesus. Even when it is trying to reject God, the world ironically worships; it cannot help itself. The very stones cry out. Pilate cannot help himself; he postures and persecutes, but, like Pharaoh of old, he achieves nothing other than magnifying the saving power of God. He cannot help himself; he literally cannot help himself. Only the one who stands before him accused can truly help him. Somewhere in his soul, he senses this. Pilate the cowardly bureaucrat believes that his salvation depends upon political finesse; Pilate the human being stares into the face of Jesus Christ and instinctively knows that "his hope is built on nothing less."

Psychologist Paul Pruyser once wrote of the awkwardness that is often felt at the end of a 50-minute therapy session. The counselee feels it; the therapist feels it. There is no good way to end; something is missing. Pruyser suggests that what is missing, perhaps, is the benediction. "Could a nervous giggle, a great hesitancy in parting at termination, or a tendency to drag the hour on beyond its formal end be interpreted as a nonverbal demand for a . . . blessing?"[2] Here in a secular therapeutic environment, there is the hunger to close with more than a "so — we'll see you next time," but with a blessing. The secular cannot keep the sacred out; the world, like Pilate, ironically worships even when it is trying to rid itself of God.

Before Jesus was brought to Pilate, the Pharisees had watched the crowd gathering around Jesus and scowled ironically, "You see, you can do nothing. Look, the world has gone after him!" (John 12:19). With this complaint, they inadvertently proclaimed the gospel: The powers-that-be can do nothing; from Christ's fullness, the world will receive grace upon grace and will finally follow him. And there, perhaps, leading the prayers of the creed, will be old Pontius himself.

---

1. One of the best descriptions of the seven-fold dramatic and chiastic structure of this story in John can be found in Raymond Brown, *The Death*

Of The Messiah: From Gethsemane To The Grave, Volume 1 (New York: Doubleday, 1994), pp. 757-759.

2. Paul Pruyser, "The Master Hand: Psychological Notes on Pastoral Blessing," in William B. Oglesby, Jr., editor, *The New Shape Of Pastoral Theology* (Nashville and New York: Abingdon Press, 1969), p. 357.

Easter
John 20:1-18 (C, L)
John 20:1-9 (RC)

Running Around The Empty Tomb

According to the Gospel of John, the very earliest response to the event of the resurrection was not praise, stark terror, ecstatic dancing, paralyzed fear, unbridled joy, speechless astonishment, or exultant song — but running. Yes, running. In the early morning hours of the first day of the week, as it begins to crack across human consciousness that something utterly unexpected and world-shifting has occurred out there in the garden cemetery, the first people who experience this event react by running ... running all over the place.

First, there is Mary Magdalene. In the quiet darkness just before dawn, she makes her way to the burial place of Jesus. She is the first to encounter the great surprise of the empty tomb, but this does not enable her to believe in the resurrection — that will come later (John 20:11-18). In the pre-dawn shadows, the empty tomb does not raise Mary's hope in the new life of the risen Christ; rather, it deepens her sadness over the death of her friend Jesus.

But even though the empty tomb does not strengthen her faith, it does increase her velocity. She picks up her heels and runs, sprinting away from the tomb to tell two of Jesus' disciples, Peter and the beloved disciple, how someone has taken away the body of their Lord and how the sad news about Jesus has gotten even sadder. Peer, then, into the shadows of Easter's first moment and see there a strange sight — Mary Magdalene in a breakneck dash away from the garden. As an old saying of the French Foreign Legion has it: "When in doubt, gallop."

But Mary is not the only one dashing about in the Easter story. When she gets to Peter and the beloved disciple, she no sooner gets her story out of her mouth than they, too, break out running. At first, they are both running *toward* something, running with amazement toward the source of their incredulity, legs pumping, breathing hard, faces flushed, running toward the empty tomb, running toward the gaping hole in the universe of human expectation left by the absent body of Jesus.

But gradually, John tells us, instead of simply running toward the tomb they also begin to run *against* each other. Turning their eyes away from the finish line and glancing enviously at each other, the adrenaline kicks in, and the mad and mutual dash turns into a footrace. The companions in sorrow become competitors on the track, Peter versus the other disciple, the pressure of the contest pushing their aching muscles to the limit as they rush along, vying for God knows what.

In fact, only God does truly know what they strive for in this mad dash. Indeed, why is everyone in this story running? At one level, of course, the answer is obvious. Mary, Peter and the beloved disciple would probably say that the reason why they have greeted this first Easter with instantaneous wind sprints is because of the fear and the excitement of it all, because they sensed intuitively that the moment was filled with electricity, dread and urgency. Like people who have been startled by a sudden, sharp clap of thunder on a clear, blue day, they did not immediately know exactly what had happened, but they spontaneously responded by jumping up and letting their feet fly. Whatever it meant that the tomb was astonishingly empty, it surely meant they could not sit still, so they ran.

But that does not explain why Peter and the beloved disciple suddenly turned their jog into a track meet. If one pressed them a bit, they might sheepishly confess that they were running not only because they were excited and awestruck but also because they were — might as well admit it — rivals. They started running out of exhilaration, but then competition between them took over, and they wanted to beat each other to the tomb.

All through John's Gospel, Peter (the leader of the disciples) and the beloved disciple (the one who seems to be closest to the heart of Jesus) are natural rivals for center stage. When they heard Mary's word and began running, no doubt all that mattered to them initially was the news that the tomb was empty; but as they ran, the old rivalry clicked into place, and, matching stride for stride, it began to count who got there first.

But even this does not plumb the depths of their running. They may be running because they are excited, and they may be running because they are rivals, but the writer of John sees something much more profound in their footrace. John believes that these two disciples are not merely racing toward a vacant grave; though they do not yet know it, they are running toward the future, toward the resurrection, toward a radical new way of life. When they started running, they were the pupils of a dead teacher; by the time their running is done, they will be the disciples of a risen and living Christ.

So, when John reports that the beloved disciple "outran Peter and reached the tomb first" (John 20:4), he is not simply reporting the results of the heat, he is making a theological statement. John wants to say that the beloved disciple is the first person to arrive at *Easter*, the first person to believe in the good news of the resurrection, the first child of the kingdom to wake up and see the dawn of the new creation.

Why is it important to know that the beloved disciple won the race? Why is John concerned to report that this disciple took a running jump and became the first human being to leap across the chasm between the old and dying age and the season of God's triumph? The reason is that the beloved disciple is first not only in foot speed, but first also in the *way* he came to believe. His way of believing in the resurrection is, in John's view, the primary and essential way of believing.

83

Others will come to belief, but not like the beloved disciple. Mary will believe when she actually sees the risen Christ and hears him call her name. The other disciples, save Thomas, will believe when Jesus appears to them saying, "Peace be with you." And as for Thomas, he will come to belief when the risen Jesus comes to him and offers to let him touch his hands and side.

But the beloved disciple is different. He believes when he sees . . . nothing. He does not see Jesus; he does not touch Jesus; he does not hear Jesus call his name. He just peers into the empty tomb and believes. In other words, the beloved disciple, unlike the others, believes in the resurrection in the light of Jesus' *absence*. He has no evidence, save the emptiness. He has no proofs, no photographs, no scorched places on the earth caused by a burst of resurrection energy. He doesn't even have straight the biblical background on all this. All he has is an empty place where the body of the one who loved him used to be. But it is enough: "He saw and believed" (John 20:8).

Now we can understand why, from John's point of view, it was so important to record who won that footrace to the tomb. John wants us to know that the very first believer in the resurrection, the forerunner of all Easter faith, came to belief in precisely the same way that you and I do — *not* seeing the risen Jesus. The risen Jesus has not appeared to us in a garden and called our name. The risen Jesus has not found us and stretched out his wounded hands for us to touch. The Easter faith is not only "He is risen!" but also "He is not here." The resurrection of Christ means the absence of Jesus of Nazareth, and the beloved disciple was the first to know that, and the first to believe.

"Blessed are those who have not seen," Jesus said, "and yet have come to believe." By this, he means us, of course, and the beloved disciple, who believed though he did not see, is our forerunner.

The beloved disciple believed in the resurrection when he saw the empty tomb not because he was a mystic or a psychic but because he knew and trusted Jesus. An infant will cry out in fear when his mother leaves his sight, but eventually there comes a day when the mother goes to the next room, out of the infant's sight, and yet the child is not afraid and does not cry. The mother's love has moved from being only an external reality to being an inner certainty. The child now trusts that the mother's absence is not abandonment but a different expression of love. Just so, when the beloved disciple saw the empty place where his Master had been, when he realized that Jesus was out of his sight, he did not fear abandonment; Jesus' love had become for him an inner certainty, and he bet his life on the wager that this absence was another and even higher expression of Jesus' love.

In John Updike's *A Month of Sundays,* there is a parable about how the Christian faith is, indeed, an improbable wager on the impossible possibility. In one episode, a group of men are playing a variation of poker. In this game, each person is dealt several cards, some of them on the table face up and the others concealed in the hand.

In one round, the main character, a man named Thomas, has been dealt a very strong hand, and he decides to bet heavily. As Thomas keeps sweetening the pot and raising the stakes, all of the other players drop out one by one, intimidated by Thomas' hand, that is, all except one player, a stutterer named Fred.

Curiously, Fred appears to have a poor hand; his cards showing on the table are "nondescript garbage." Astonishingly, though, he keeps up the betting pace, calling and raising Thomas at every opportunity. Thomas is puzzled since his own hand is a poker player's dream. It isn't absolutely perfect — he is holding one poor card — but other than this single little flaw his hand is virtually unbeatable. Why does Fred keep on betting against such odds? Why doesn't he fold?

When the time comes to lay down the cards, though, Thomas is shocked to discover that Fred has the winning hand. When he compares Fred's hand with his, Thomas realizes that there was only one card in the whole deck that could have made Thomas the loser, and that was the one bad card that Thomas had hidden in his hand. If Thomas had held any other card, he would have won, and won big. In other words, Fred was betting everything — everything — on the tiny chance that Thomas held this one losing card. Dumbfounded, Thomas thinks to himself:

> *Fred had stayed, then, against me when only one card in the deck . . . could have made my hand a loser to his. Two truths dawned upon me:*
> *He was crazy.*
> *He had won.*
> *He had raised not on a reasonable faith but on a virtual impossibility; and he had been right. "Y-y-y-you didn't feel to me like you had it," he told me, raking it in.*[1]

The beloved disciple goes to the tomb and finds it empty. No body, no visions, no explanation. Just a vacant tomb. This is a poor hand, to be sure, and the world has much stronger cards showing. But the beloved disciple wagers everything anyway. He bets his life on a virtual impossibility, that Jesus' absence was the sign of a new and radiant presence, that Jesus had been raised from the dead. There is but one combination of cards that could make him a winner, and he stakes everything on that possibility. Now, we know two truths about him: He is crazy — a fool for Christ — and he has won. Jesus has indeed been raised from the dead.

And so we believe today, too. Not because of proofs or evidence, but because the beloved disciple knew and trusted Jesus and we do, too. The beloved disciple told the story of the empty tomb and the risen Christ to others, and they believed it, as well. Then they told the story to still others, and those others passed this great wonder along, down a great chain of believing all the way to us. And we wager everything.

Clint Tidwell is the pastor of a church in a small Southern town, and one of his blessings — and one of his curses — is that the 80-year-old owner and still-active editor of the local newspaper is a member of his congregation. The blessing part is that this old journalist believes Tidwell to be one of the finest preachers around, and, wishing the whole town to benefit from this homiletical wisdom, he publishes a summary of Tidwell's Sunday sermon every Monday morning in the paper. The curse part is that this newspaperman, though well meaning, is a bit on the dotty and eccentric side, and Tidwell is often astonished to read the synopses of his sermons. The man owns the newspaper; nobody dares edit his columns, and the difference between what Tidwell thought he said and what the editor actually heard is often a source of profound amazement and embarrassment to Tidwell.

Tidwell's deepest amazement and embarrassment, however, came not when the newspaper editor misunderstood the Sunday sermon but, to the contrary, when he understood it all too sharply and clearly. It was early on the Monday morning after Easter, and Tidwell, in his bathrobe and slippers, was padding out the carport door to retrieve the Monday newspaper. The paper was lying at the end of the driveway, and, as Tidwell approached, he could see that the morning headline was in "second coming" sized type. What could it be? he wondered. Had war broken out somewhere? Had the local bank failed over the weekend? Had a cure for cancer been discovered? As he drew close enough to focus on the headline, he was startled to read the words, "Tidwell Claims Jesus Christ Rose From The Dead."

A red flush crept up Tidwell's neck. Yes, of course, he had claimed in yesterday's sermon that Christ rose from the dead, but golly, was that headline news? What would the neighbors think? I mean, you're supposed to say that on Easter, aren't you, that Christ rose from the dead, but that's not like saying that some person who died last week had risen from the grave, is it? Suddenly, as he looked at the screaming headline, what had been a routine Easter sermon had Tidwell feeling rather foolish.

Indeed, it is foolish — the foolishness of the gospel. Those who gather on this Easter Day to sing and say that "Jesus Christ is Risen Today" do so not because we have proved anything philosophically, discerned some mystical key to the

Scripture, or found some unassailable piece of historical evidence. We believe in the resurrection because the beloved disciple, the forerunner of all Easter faith, believed and passed the word along all the way into the present, prompting frail folks, like Tidwell and like us, to say what we believe: "I believe in Jesus Christ, born of the virgin Mary, suffered under Pontius Pilate, crucified, dead and buried. He descended into hell, and — dare we believe it? Dare we wager everything on it? — rose again on the third day."

---

1. John Updike, *A Month Of Sundays* (New York: Alfred A. Knopf, 1975), pp. 197-198.

The Church With Nothing

Check out the church ads on the religion page of the Saturday edition of most big city newspapers and you find some impressive sounding places of worship. There, with sleek graphics and Madison Avenue phrases, a few select churches boast of their assets — their choirs, their friendliness, their powerful preaching, their singles ministries, their ample parking, their family life centers, their sensitive child care, and their compassionate spirit. Some churches, it seems, have it all.

Other churches, however, appear by contrast to have nothing, absolutely nothing. Take, for example, the church depicted in our text for today. Here, we get our first glimpse of the disciples gathered together after the resurrection, the first glimpse, in other words, of the church in its earliest days, and, all in all, it is not a very pretty picture. Near the end of his life, Jesus had carefully prepared his disciples to be a devoted and confident fellowship of faith. They were to be a community of profound love with the gates wide open and the welcome mat always out, but here we find them barricaded in a house with the doors bolted shut. They were to be the kind of people who stride boldly into the world to bear fruit in Jesus' name, a people full of the Holy Spirit performing even greater works than Jesus himself (John 14:12), but here we find them cowering in fear, hoping nobody will find out where they are before they get their alibis straight. In short, we see here the church at its worst — scared, disheartened and defensive. If this little sealed-off group of Christians were to place one of those cheery church ads in the Saturday newspaper, what could it possibly say? "The friendly church where all are welcome"? Hardly, unless one counts locked doors as a sign of hospitality. "The church with a warm heart and a bold mission"? Actually more like the church with sweaty palms and a timid spirit.

Indeed, John's gospel gives us a snapshot of a church with nothing — no plan, no promise, no program, no perky youth ministry, no powerful preaching, no parking lot, nothing. In fact, when all is said and done, this terrified little band huddled in the corner of a room with a chair braced against the door has only one thing going for it: the risen Christ. And that seems to be the main point of this story. In the final analysis, this is a story about how the risen Christ pushed open the bolted door of a church with nothing, how the risen Christ enters the fearful chambers of every church and fills the place with his own life.

What we are asked to recognize, of course, is that every church is finally this way; every church, no matter what it says about itself in the newspaper, if it is left to its own devices, if it draws only upon its own resources, is nothing. No liturgical mascara, no programmatic cosmetic, can conceal for long the fact that, apart from the presence of the risen Christ, the church is an empty place.

Take the matter of worship leadership. Worship leaders either know that mystery resides at the core of worship, or they don't — and congregations can tell the difference. Congregations can sense whether their leaders truly believe that they are in the presence of mystery or not. If a worship leader is genuinely convinced that worship is taking place in the power of the Spirit and at the foot of the burning bush, then no matter how homespun and halting the liturgy may be, that energizing truth cannot be hid. If, on the other hand, the worship leader is convinced that the only spirit at work is the human spirit and the only things moving in the sanctuary are the offering plates, then no matter how lofty the liturgy, poetic the prayers or polished the sermon, the fearful emptiness of the moment cannot be concealed.

I was recently a part of a congregation that was victimized by a worship leader who, since he evidently perceived God to be absent, felt it an obligation to make up for this lack by talking incessantly through the Lord's Supper. He prattled his way along, trying to transform the worship service into a "meaningful worship experience" by the sheer force of his personality. He quoted Scripture with a syrupy tone and told cute stories and oozed out pious bromides. In essence, he betrayed his conviction that nothing was happening here except himself, no dynamism in this worship except his own energy. There we were, the church, locked in a room, bolted behind his egotistic lack of faith.

Sometimes churches begin to think of themselves as useful social institutions in and of themselves. No one would say it out loud, of course, but the attitude hangs in the air that, sure, this is a place where God is worshipped, but if God were somehow to disappear from the scene, the church would still be a fine character-building contribution to the physical and emotional well-being of the community.

John's gospel pulls the skin off of this illusion. If we want to see what becomes of the church when it is deprived of its central holy presence, look at this picture of the disciples huddled defensively in a darkened room, peeking anxiously through the drapes to make sure the world isn't after them. In the absence of God, the church is hollow, empty of meaning and purpose, fearfully locked behind its own institutional facade. Indeed, the ceaseless and frenetic activity of many congregations — with programs ranging from "Mother's Morning Out" to "Fitness for Faith" — is often only the lonely attempt to fill in the void where God, "the most missed of all missing persons,"[1] should be.

The good news is that into the midst of this void, into the center of this fearful church with nothing, the risen Christ came and said, "Peace be with you" (John 20:19). It is into the emptiness of their community — and ours — into the vacuum of confidence, into the void of discipleship that Jesus comes to fill the vacant space with his peace.

What Jesus says to the church is remarkable. Given the circumstances, we may have expected that the risen Christ would come with a scold. "Shame on you for your fear and failure. I sent you into the world, not into a locked closet. Now go!" Or perhaps the risen Christ would come to bail out these terrified incompetents and take over the task himself. "You obviously can't handle the job. I give you a divine mission, but here you are, only hours after I leave, in a hideout shaking in your boots. I'll take it from here."

But no, Jesus neither scolds nor relieves them of their duty. To this church with nothing, Jesus provides a strange set of words and actions, a string of seeming *non sequiturs*. He says "Peace be with you"; he shows them his hands and his side; he says again, "Peace be with you"; he tells them that he is sending them into the world, just as he, Jesus, was sent; he breathes on them, saying, "Receive the Holy Spirit"; and he commissions them to perform binding acts of forgiveness.

To our eyes, this is an odd collection of sayings and deeds. But to the earliest readers of the Gospel of John, their meaning would be clear. Each of the things that Jesus said and did is a clear symbol of some aspect of the church's life. "Peace be with you" comes straight from the liturgy, from Sunday worship. Likewise, being shown Jesus' hands and side, Jesus' body, is a reference to the Lord's Supper, and the breathing of the Holy Spirit comes from the early church's practice of baptism. Being sent is, of course, the church's mission, and forgiving sins is the texture of the church's inner life of fellowship and reconciliation.

Put them all together, and what this means is that the risen Christ comes to call the church to be the church. He comes to the church with nothing and gives it everything, provides it with what it needs truly to be the church: worship, mission, and forgiveness. Without his presence, there is cowering fear. In his presence there is open praise, bold mission, and healed community.

Theologian Karl Barth once remarked that to say the old line from the creed, "I believe in the Holy Catholic Church" does not mean that we believe in the church. It means rather to believe that God is present and at work in the church, that "in this assembly, the work of the Holy Spirit takes place. ... We do not believe in the Church: but we do believe that in this congregation the work of the Holy Spirit becomes an event."[2]

Barth's words rang true for me some years ago, when I was invited by a church in a nearby town to be the worship leader at a special evening communion service. The church staff had planned this service to be educational as well as worshipful. The idea was that, first, the congregation would gather in the sanctuary and I would give a brief talk about the meanings of the Lord's Supper. Then, we would go into the fellowship hall and be seated around tables for the service itself.

At each table there would be the flour and other ingredients to form the dough for the communion loaves. The plan called for each table to prepare a loaf and, while the loaves baked in the ovens of the church kitchen, the people at each table were to engage in various exercises designed to get them talking about their experiences in the faith.

It was a good idea, but like many well-planned events, things looked better on the drawing board than they turned out in reality. There were problems. Children at many tables began to play in the baking ingredients, and white clouds of flour floated around the room coating everybody and everything. There were delays in the kitchen, and the communion bread baked with agonizing slowness. Some of the tables ran out of things to say; children grew weary and fussy; the room was filled with commotion and restlessness. The planners had dreamed of an event of excitement, innovation, peak learning, and moving worship. What happened was noise, exhaustion, and people making the best of a difficult situation.

In other words, despite the rosy plans, it was the real church worshipping down there in the church basement.

Finally, the service ended, and, with no little relief, I was able to pronounce the benediction. "The peace of Christ be with you all," I said, and just as I did, a child's voice from somewhere in the room called out strong and true, "It already is."

Just that — "It already is" — but with those words the service was transformed into an event of joy and holy mystery. That small voice captured what the Gospel of John is trying to say. In the midst of a church that can claim nothing for itself, a church of noise, confusion, weariness, and even fear, the risen Christ comes to give peace. The peace of Christ be with you? Because the risen Christ comes to inhabit our empty places, then, as the child said, "It already is," and the church with nothing becomes the church with everything.

---

1. A phrase for which I am indebted to Frederick Buechner.

2. Karl Barth, *Dogmatics In Outline* (New York: Harper Torchbooks, 1959), pp. 142-143.

Getting Down To The Local Issues

"The landscape of politics is changing," explained the political pundit on the television talk show. His hands were outstretched in front of him, palms up, as if to say, "We may as well face it."

"It's the impact of the instant, electronic media," he continued. "Two generations ago, a presidential candidate could write one speech addressing the big issues facing the nation and whistle stop around the country giving it everywhere. But not today. The issues are hotter and more immediate. People don't care about anything in the general sense, not the broad economy, not health care in the abstract, not education in the global sense. They want to know about *their* factory, *their* jobs, *their* health benefits, *their* neighborhood school, *their* personal sense of values. The candidate who hopes to win cannot run around speaking vaguely about some generic American dream. To get the vote, you have to get down to the local issues."

It was a point well taken — the importance of getting down to the local issues. Most of the time, it would seem, politicians need to learn a few things from the church, but perhaps here is a case where the church needs to learn a lesson from the politicians. "I believe in God, the Father Almighty, maker of heaven and earth ...," intones the Sunday congregation, but what does that have to do with the local issues? "I believe in Jesus Christ, his only Son, our Lord ...," the chant continues, but how does this connect to the woman in the choir whose cancer has just returned after years of remission, the 17-year-old anxiously trying to decide what to do with his life, the young attorney who is seeing unethical practices at her firm, the man who at age 55 just lost his job, or the plant manager who had to make the decision to lay him off? "On the third day, he rose again from the dead ..." say the unison voices, but how does this connect to the man who, every Sunday afternoon, places fresh flowers on the grave of his wife? What does the Easter faith have to do with the local issues?

For many people, the Christian faith seems to float above the gritty circumstances of life, disconnected from the "local issues." Such people are not opposed to the idea that God is good, loving, and merciful, and they do not hesitate to say "on the third day he was raised again from the dead." But these are distant truths. The problem is not that the faith is incredible; the problem is that it is not applicable. The gospel seems to them to be vaguely true, but it is a tractionless truth. They affirm the faith in the same way they are able to affirm that the planet Venus is 67 million miles from the sun. Trustworthy information, to be sure, but not much help in planning the day.

Specifically, then, what difference does it make in the ins and outs of everyday life; what difference does it make in the way we work, play, vote, spend money, make decisions, love or hate, change direction or hold steady the course, and make the hundreds of choices, large and small, that make up the fabric of our lives; what difference does it make to all this that on a Sunday morning two millennia ago an itinerant preacher named Jesus of Nazareth was not found in the tomb where he had been buried a few days before? In other words, what does the Easter faith have to do with the local issues?

In the early 1970s, a group of church leaders gathered over the course of several months to plan a national conference, which they decided to give the festive name "A Celebration of Evangelism." The choice of the word "celebration" was no accident since they wanted the spirit of the conference to be positive and upbeat, emphasizing the sunnier side of Christianity. After several blue sky meetings, however, one of the planning team, a minister from Chicago, disturbed the optimistic mood by saying, "Despite our happy talk, I have in my congregation a 30-year-old man just diagnosed with melanoma. Just before I left home for this meeting, a couple I have been counseling for two years told me that they were giving up and filing for divorce. Five young men in my congregation are in Vietnam fighting a war they do not understand, and one of them is my own son. Now, I hope by the end of this conference I will be celebrating with you, but if you think I am celebrating now, you are wrong." In a church ready to open the hymnbook and sing the alleluias, this man was issuing a warning that Easter is no genuine celebration unless it touches the private wounds and the tragedies near-at-hand. In short, Easter is not truly good news until it gets down to the local issues.

That is the beauty of Luke's story of the two disciples trudging their weary way down the Emmaus road. When all is said and done, this is a story about how the truth of Easter belongs not only on the front page of the newspaper but also on the back page, nestled among the items of neighborhood news. This is a story of how the cosmic truth of Christ's resurrection comes home as a local issue.

As the story goes, two otherwise unknown followers of Jesus are traveling the seven dusty miles from Jerusalem to the village of Emmaus. As the camera pans dramatically across the scene, we see that this day is Easter, the first day of the new creation, the day God shattered the chains of evil and broke the icy grip of death by raising Jesus from the tomb, the day human history shifted on its axis. On this day, every valley has been lifted up, every mountain has been made low, and a great highway of redemption has appeared in the wilderness of human brokenness. But as the camera moves in for a close-up, we realize that the Emmaus road is not a highway; it is a village lane, a local thoroughfare. And to these disheartened followers of Jesus, it is not yet Easter; it is only Sunday afternoon, the first day of yet another week, another day in an unbroken string of days when life grinds on the way it always has. It may be the Day of Resurrection on the cosmic plane, but Easter has not yet become a local issue.

A stranger catches up to them on the road, a stranger with a face like all faces. He is, of course, the risen Christ, the bright morning star of God's new day, but in the dimness of their discouragement they cannot recognize him. If we jump ahead to the end of the story, however, by the time they have reached Emmaus, their hearts are burning with faith and they are joyfully rushing back to Jerusalem singing the Easter hymn, "The Lord has risen indeed!" Easter has moved from a ripple on the far edge of the universe to a local event.

What happened? How did the great and sweeping truth of Easter become a local issue on the back road to Emmaus? The crucial clue is found — as crucial clues often are — at the end of the story. "Then they told what had happened on the road," Luke narrates, "and how he had been made known to them in the breaking of bread" (Luke 24:35). Easter becomes a local issue on the road ... and in the breaking of bread.

The first readers of Luke would have smiled at this reminder that Easter became a local issue on the road, for they knew about the road. The "road" was more than a highway; it was a symbol for them of the whole Christian life, of the path of mission laid out before them. In fact, these early Christians were called, by friends and enemies alike, "the Way" — in other words, they were nicknamed "people of the road" (see Acts 9:2).

So, in a literal sense the risen Christ became a local issue on the road to Emmaus, but, in a deeper sense, the truth here is that the resurrection comes home as the church travels down the "Way," down the road of mission, putting one foot in front of another as it walks every day along the way of obedience to the gospel. As we work for peace in our families,

98

seek reconciliation in our towns, visit those who are sick, comfort those who are distressed, welcome the stranger, teach the faith to our children, speak the good news to those who do not know it, whisper encouragement to those who doubt, provide food for the hungry, and do the thousands of everyday acts of obedience that make up the Christian life, it is here along this road that the risen Lord comes to meet us.

In *The Spiritual Life Of Children,* Robert Coles writes about Ginny, a young girl from a poor family who is bright, articulate, imaginative and has a keenly developed spirituality. Ginny recounts, for example, that her uncle, who was wounded in Vietnam, is still nervous and upset, prone to frequent crying, and she wonders how God must have felt during the violence of that war. "If my uncle cries now," she reflects, "God must have cried, too. He must have *wept.* Don't you think?"

One day, Ginny was walking home and along the way encountered an elderly woman who seemed lost and confused. Ginny asked the woman if she needed help, and the woman, with relief, responded "If you could, that would be wonderful." Ginny discovered that the woman had been walking to visit her daughter, but had gotten disoriented. She showed Ginny the written directions she had, and Ginny knew immediately where she had gotten lost and where she needed to go. Although Ginny was now late for her home chores, she sensed that getting this troubled stranger safely to her destination was the chore she most needed to be doing. So she traveled with her, talked gently to her, listened to her as the woman spoke of the pain in her life, and guided her to her daughter's house.

When they arrived and Ginny started to leave, the woman grasped her arm and announced that God had sent Ginny to her and that later she would pray a prayer of thanks to God for having Ginny there. The woman then gave Ginny a kiss.

On the way home, Ginny wondered what it would be like to be old, wondered if she were old and in need if God would send some kid like her to help. "Maybe God puts you here," Ginny thought, "and . . . gives you these hints of what's ahead, and you should pay attention to them, because that's Him speaking to you."[1]

There on the "road," as a little girl helped a stranger in need, performing the chore she knew most needed to be done, the presence of God became a local issue.

But it was not just "on the road" that the Emmaus event happened; it was also "in the breaking of bread." The first readers of Luke would have smiled at that, too, for they also knew about "the breaking of bread." This was their way of speaking of worship, especially the Lord's Supper. Indeed, as they read again and again this Emmaus Road story, they would have been amazed to see glimmers of their Sunday worship woven into the narrative: the creed (Luke 24:19-24), the sermon (Luke 24:27), and the Eucharist (Luke 24:30) are all there. When one knows how to look, one can see the Emmaus story as a narrative version of Luke's Sunday bulletin! In sum, Easter becomes a local issue in worship.

A woman spoke quietly of the death of her father. He had been a proud man, she said, a man who spent all his work days tilling the soil of a Carolina farm and all his sabbaths praising God for life and seed and family. A final bout with cancer sent him to the hospital never to come home again, and in the last week of his life the disease provided the added indignity of a stroke that robbed him of his speech. As his family visited his bedside, his eyes would moisten with frustration and grief as he tried in vain to speak to these people he loved so dearly.

On his last day alive, the attending physician had issued the signal, the family had gathered in his room — the daughter and her two brothers. With strength fading, the father motioned to his son that he wanted a glass of water. The son hastened to the sink and returned with a full water glass, which he held toward his father's lips. But the old man pushed the glass away and moved his finger from the glass toward his son, as if to say, "You drink it."

Hesitant and uncertain, the son lifted the glass to his lips and drank from it. Then the father motioned toward his

100

daughter, indicating that she should drink some, too. Sensing what his father wanted, the son passed the glass to his sister, and she drank. Now the father, pointed toward the other son, and the daughter realized what was happening. "He is serving communion," she gasped.

There in the face of death, this father summoned a sacramental water glass to administer the feast of life. There is a wordless act of worship, the promise of the resurrection came home.

On the road and in the place of worship, the great parabola of grace touches the near edge of life, and Easter becomes a very local issue.

---

1. Robert Coles, *The Spiritual Life Of Children* (Boston: Houghton Mifflin, 1990), pp. 332-334.

.

Easter 4
John 10:1-10

Knowing The Voice

The dinner party had gone well. It was the kind of evening when good food was matched by rich conversation and warm cheer. As the dishes were being cleared and cream was being stirred into after-dinner coffee, the conversation took a more serious turn.

The guest of honor was a church leader from central Europe, the Soviet Union had come apart only months before, and the table was filled with eager questions. How had the church in his country fared during the long Soviet frost? What changes were occurring now that the warmer winds of democracy were blowing across central Europe? What wisdom did his experience bring for the church in North America?

He spoke slowly — even cautiously — at first, measuring his words, weighing their risk, a man unaccustomed to candor among relative strangers. Gradually gaining confidence, he spoke of dramatic shifts in the social and political climate of his region, of the church made strong through hardship and persecution. Indeed, with an eye cast toward the American religious scene, he observed that possibly the greatest threat to the church in his own land was the temptation to relax its guard in the new atmosphere of freedom, that the church could lose its sense of call by falling into an easy alliance with a seemingly friendlier culture.

He told about the days under totalitarianism, how the church was officially tolerated but always undermined and repressed, how the clergy were always monitored by secret agents who had infiltrated their ranks. "We would have a meeting about some matter of church business," he said, "knowing for certain that not everyone seated at the table could be trusted; some of the 'ministers' present were, in fact, government agents." He paused for a moment and then added, "But even though these government spies were careful never to betray their true identities, we could always tell who they were."

"But how?" someone asked.

"The voice," he replied. "The voice. Something in their voices would give them away."

The voice. The words may have been smooth and well-chosen, but there was something in the texture of the voice that disclosed the agent of deception, the wolf in sheep's clothing. There was something in the voice that revealed the distinction between the true and the false, between the dependable and the treacherous. "Something in their voices," he said, "would give them away."

In a similar way, Jesus himself said that his own followers could divide the trustworthy from the untrustworthy by the sound of a voice. "They are like sheep who will not follow a stranger," he said, "because a stranger's voice they do not know. The sheep know the voice of their shepherd, and they follow only him." Because they belong to Jesus, the Good Shepherd, they respond faithfully to the sound of his voice and his voice alone.

What is it about a voice that signals a trust? What is there about Jesus' voice that beckons his own to follow? The world is cluttered with voices competing for our attention. A cacophony of voices shout for our loyalty, urge us to get into step and to join the followers of this or that bumper-stickered cause: "Have you hugged your child today?" "Support the NRA," "Christians for Choice," "Pro-life Christians," "Save the

Rain Forests," "Buy American," "Question Authority," "Promote Family Values," "Fight Taxes," "Worship Next Sunday," "Work for Justice," "Boycott Lettuce." Jesus' voice may sometimes be heard *above* these clamoring voices, and it may be heard *in* some of them, but Jesus claims that his followers will surely know his voice when they hear it, that they will be able to distinguish his clear and true call from the false tones of strangers. But what makes this so? What is there about Jesus' voice that is unmistakable to his followers?

Part of it, of course, is familiarity. Even a young child, the crib surrounded by whispering and beckoning voices, turns and brightens at the sound of the one voice most familiar, the one voice most trusted, the intimate voice of the mother. Or again, two people meet, seemingly for the first time. They are cautious, wary, as strangers are at initial encounter. But then one speaks a word of greeting and there is the flicker, then the flame, of astonishing recognition. "Is that you?" exclaims the other, arms opening for an embrace. "Is that really you? How many years has it been? How we've changed, you and I. I didn't recognize your face, but your voice . . . I would know your voice anywhere."

Just so, Jesus' followers recognize his voice because his voice is familiar. They discern its cadences; they remember its reassuring rhythms. Over and again, in times of distress and pain, when they have not been sure that they could take one more step along the pathway of suffering, he has spoken comfort to them: "Peace I leave with you; my peace I give to you. I do not give to you as the world gives. Do not let your hearts be troubled, and do not let them be afraid" (John 14:27). Many times when their faith has faltered and their vision grown dim, he has reassured them: "Do not let your hearts be troubled. Believe in God, believe also in me" (John 14:1). When they were uncertain of life's purpose, confused about what makes life good and true, he has called them anew: "This is my commandment, that you love one another as I have loved you" (John 15:12). Even when they have stood at the rim of death's canyon, staring with grief into its violet depths, over and over he has spoken to them of hope: "I am the resurrection and the life. Those who believe in me, even though they die, will live ..." (John 11:25).

At every bend in the road, in every predicament along the way, they have felt Jesus' presence and have heard his familiar words; all the days of their lives he has been the Good Shepherd, and they know his voice. In the flurry of voices that fill the world, the followers of Jesus listen for the sound of the voice they know best, the voice that speaks compassionately, mercifully, lovingly and hopefully. When they hear this voice — but only this voice — they follow; they do not respond to the voices of strangers, the voices of bitterness, judgment, hatred and strife.

But it is more than familiarity that causes the followers of Jesus to recognize his voice. Jesus "calls his sheep by name and leads them out." The voice of Jesus speaks personally and commandingly. The voice of Jesus is not spoken over a public address system, making a vague general announcement for all the world to hear. The voice of Jesus speaks to each one, lovingly calls out each name, summoning each and every person to follow.

Not long ago a friend told me about a church drama troupe that presented, as a special event on the weekend before Christmas, a "dessert and drama" production of Charles Dickens' classic *A Christmas Carol*. The church fellowship hall was transformed into a theater, folding chairs clustered around tables, all facing a makeshift stage fitted with painted backdrops of the tenements and sooty chimneys of nineteenth century London.

When the audience gathered and were handed their programs, some were amused to note that the part of the tightfisted Ebenezer Scrooge was being played by the chairman of the church board, a gentle man of quite un-Scrooge-like generosity. They were impressed, though, by the skill and energy he brought to his part. He growled his way through the opening scenes, ringing out every "Bah! Humbug!" with miserly ill will. He shivered with fright and dreadful self-recognition as he was encountered by the series of Christmas ghosts.

The final scene called for a transformed and jubilant Scrooge to chase the shadows of the remorseful night and to greet the light of Christmas day by flinging open his bedroom window and bellowing festively to the startled city street below, "Me-e-r-rr-y Christmas, everyone! Me-e-r-rr-y Christmas!" Then Scrooge, wishing to bestow Christmas gifts upon the needy of London and looking for someone to help dispense his cheer, was to act as if he had spied a street urchin passing by. "Hey you, boy, you there!" the mirthful Scrooge was to shout, pointing vigorously at this imaginary figure. "Come up here, boy. I've got something wonderful for you to do!"

But something beautiful and unexpected happened. When the radiant and transformed Scrooge beckoned from the window "Come up here, boy, I've got something wonderful for you to do," a six-year-old boy in the audience, seated with his family who were members of the congregation, spontaneously rose from his chair in response to this jubilant and generous call and walked on stage, ready to do "something wonderful."

The actor playing Scrooge blinked in disbelief. There was now an unscripted child from the audience standing on center stage. What to do? The audience held its breath. Then the person of faith beneath the veneer of Scrooge took charge. Bounding down from his window perch, he strode across the stage and cheerily embraced the waiting boy. "Yes, indeed," he exclaimed, his voice full of blessing. "You are the one, the *very* one I had in mind." Then he gently led the boy back to his seat in the audience, returned to the stage and resumed the play. When the curtain calls were held, it was, of course, this boy, the one who had felt himself personally summoned from his seat, who received, along with old Ebenezer himself, the audience's loudest and warmest applause.[1]

Just so, the sheep hear and know the merciful voice of the Good Shepherd, and when they get up out of their seats in the darkened auditorium and bound upon the stage ready to follow, the Good Shepherd himself embraces them. "Yes, yes, you are the one, the *very* one I had in mind."

---

1. I am indebted to the Rev. Charles Williamson of Monroe, North Carolina, for this story.

Easter 5
John 14:1-14 (C)
John 14:1-12 (L, RC)

The Way, The Truth, And The Life Style

I was amused the other day to pick up a newspaper in a faraway town and to read a feature article about a minor official in the local county government. A reporter had interviewed the deputy assistant director of the water authority or some similar civil servant, and the resulting article included a number of fairly predictable and humdrum quotes about some recent changes in the water system, the official's selfless commitment to public service, his goal of improved water quality and the like.

What was so amusing, however, was not the article itself but the accompanying color box, a small town imitation of a *USA Today* feature, showcasing selected tidbits from this fellow's private life. It was a local version of the "Dewar's Scotch Profile," and it treated this water department bureaucrat as if he were a rock star or a matinee idol. It supplied such fascinating facts as this man's "role model" (Abraham Lincoln), his "latest book read" (something by Robert Ludlum), his "drink of choice" (Corona beer, with lime), his "prime leisure activity" (tennis), his "personal clothing store" (the men's department at Sears), his "favorite musical performer" (Bruce Springsteen) and his "current wheels" (a brown 1985 Olds Cutlass).

Whether this local official rejoiced in his sudden and unexpected celebrity or was embarrassed by the billboarding of the rather commonplace facets of his fairly conventional existence, I do not know. But the fact that the newspaper was at least as interested in the superficialities of his personal life as it was in his public role does seem to point to a cultural fascination with "life styles."

A "life style" is a carefully assembled set of personal choices. It is the blend of our preferences in clothing, automobiles, books, recreation, music, food, and other aspects of the way we consume ideas and things. Something either does or does not "fit into our life style," which is put together with an interior decorator's eye for total effect. Life style magazines and programs like *Life Styles Of The Rich And Famous* allow us to monitor the choices we have made, to compare them to those who are more tasteful, affluent and influential, and to signal to others that we belong in their set. Indeed, we tend to seek out those whose life styles are similar to our own, herding together in what have been called "life style enclaves."[1]

What this means, of course, is that a life style is different from a life. A life style can be adjusted with a twist of the television dial, a shift in reading patterns, or the purchase of a new car. A life, on the other hand, is all of us. A life, therefore, tends to be messier than a mere life style, harder to change, and it often involves untidy facts, like a problem with alcohol, a parent in a nursing home or a child with a learning disorder. A life style, like the longest suit in a bridge hand, is composed of the cards we lead with, the ones we lay face up on the table to show our strength. A life, on the other hand, is every aspect of who we are, every card we hold, weak and strong. Renting the video of *Saturday Night Fever* is life style; staying up all Saturday night with a child with a fever is life.

Our life styles can lose luster, but with sufficient cash flow, they can be improved; our lives, on the other hand, are more desperate and in need of being saved. It is worthy of note, then, that Jesus, gathered with his disciples around the table for the last meal before his death, pointed down the road he would

110

soon be traveling and said, "I am the way, and the truth, and the life." He did not say, "I am the way, the truth, and the *life style.*"

The difference is significant. Jesus came to save all of us, to lead every bit of our human being down the road of redemption, all of the untidy, unraveled ends that compose a life. Jesus offers us life, "abundant" life (John 10:10), not a pinch of religion tossed in as a "prime leisure activity" but a life where every facet of it, the suffering as well as the joy, is the arena for God's saving grace. Our faith is not a spiritual applique among other life style features but an all-encompassing and demanding reality.

A recent college graduate, writing in *The New Yorker,* commented that, as he moved into the professional world and began to earn some money, he was feeling the tension between two cravings: to live, on the one hand, "*the* good life, full of bay windows and summer vacations and dinner out whenever," and to live, on the other hand, "*a* good life, at peace with ourselves . . . ." He was, of course, describing the tension between a "life style" and a "life," between fitting the pieces together to make a pleasing whole and finding in the whole of life that which makes for peace.

As he considered the dilemma, he cited Tolstoy's moving reflection on Jesus' Sermon on the Mount, in which Tolstoy wrote, "The antagonism between life and conscience may be moved in two ways: by a change of life or a change of conscience." Tolstoy chose to preserve his conscience; he began to live like a peasant. But such a fearsome choice, this young man admitted, was out of his reach. People in his situation, he observed, could stand the chafing between one's soul and one's life style more easily than they could face the awesome choice.

In one of the scenes in Herb Gardner's play *A Thousand Clowns,* the main character Murray is having an argument with his older brother Arnold about what really matters in life. Murray is something of a gentle social rebel with a refreshing vision of what human existence is all about. Arnold is his

111

opposite, a business executive who makes his compromises and plays by others' rules.

At one point in their exchange, Arnold says that he, unlike Murray, is realistic, willing to deal with the available world. He has no desire to change the world, just to accommodate to it. Arnold says that he does not consider himself to be an exceptional man; he has a wife and children, and "business is business." He continues:

> *You cannot convince me I am one of the bad guys. I get up, I go, I lie a little, I peddle a little, I watch the rules, I talk the talk. We ... have those offices high up there so we catch the wind and go with it, however it blows. But ... I will not apologize for it, I take pride; I am the best possible Arnold Burns.* [2]

Arnold Burns had settled for a "life style" but not a life. He had sadly persuaded himself that his quilt of shallow compromises made him "the best possible Arnold Burns." Jesus, however, calls us not to catch the drifting trade winds of culture but to set sail in the gale force winds of the Spirit, to venture into the open sea of faith where there is life.

Another difference between a life style and a life is that a life style is a matter of personal whim, a life is a matter of calling. A life style is a composite of choices. We choose the Ivy League look or the Banana Republic look; we choose a vegetarian or a steak-and-potatoes diet; we choose to be a Scotch drinker or a teetotaler, a jogger or a backgammon player.

A life, however, is not always about choice. Life takes us places and gives us experiences we would not choose. This is especially true of a life made rich in faith; such a life is not a getaway vacation but a vocation that will inevitably take us down paths not of our choosing.

"When you were younger," Jesus told Peter, "you used to fasten your own belt and to go wherever you wished." But now, Jesus said, "someone else will fasten a belt around you and take you where you do not wish to go" (John 21:18).

Jesus was speaking, John writes, of "the kind of death by which [Peter] would glorify God" (John 21:19). Being led captive to your own death is not to have much of a life style; offering one's all for the glory of God, though, is to have life, and to have it abundantly.

In his memoir about his career as a physician and a professor of medicine, Lewis Thomas recalls his early memories of Bellevue Hospital in New York City. One early morning in 1959, Thomas, just beginning his service as a medical school teacher, was hearing a report from a student, an intern at the hospital, about a patient who had spent two weeks on one of the wards with advanced pneumonia and meningitis. This young intern had been up all night, moving back and forth between the patient and the senior physicians and consultants in infectious diseases. The intern had done everything he could, everything he could think of, for the patient, but the patient had died.

Halfway through the formal presentation tears appeared in his eyes and rolled down his cheeks, and he wept while he finished. I knew that these were tears not of frustration but of grief, and I realized, for the first time, what kind of hospital I was in.[3]

This young intern had a life, not a life style, a life that sent him to situations he could not fix and to pour out his all for people he could not heal. Tears and grief would never be his life style choices; but a vocation of healing and tearful compassion will lead him to the place of peace.

"I am the way," said Jesus, "the truth and the life."

---

1. Robert Bellah *et al., Habits Of The Heart.*

2. Herb Gardner, *A Thousand Clowns,* p. 86.

3. Lewis Thomas, *The Youngest Science: Notes Of A Medicine Watcher* (New York: Viking Press, 1983), p. 135.

.

Easter 6
John 14:15-21

Whispering The Lyrics

Stashed away in a drawer somewhere around my house, now nearly forgotten, is a batch of old 45 rpm records from the '50s and early '60s. Worn and scratchy, long since outmoded by the flashy digital technology of compact discs, these primitive vinyls were once the jewels of a great treasure trove. Elvis' grinding out "Hound Dog," Buddy Holly and the Crickets' hiccuping "Peggy Sue," Chuck Berry's joyful hot licks in "Maybellene," the Coasters' slapstick *tour de force* "Charlie Brown," the mournful "Tears On My Pillow" by Little Anthony and the Imperials, the impenetrable and probably scandalous "Louie, Louie" by the Kingsmen, and the teenaged gropings of the Paris Sisters' "I Love How You Love Me" — they are all there, and more.

Here and there in this dusty stack, one can find an occasional recording by the great bluesmaster Jimmy Reed. A sharecropper's son, Reed brought the throbbing harmonica-and-guitar-driven black rhythm-and-blues of the Mississippi Delta into the popular rock-and-roll mainstream. My high school friends and I, fancying ourselves a budding rock band, would play and replay these recordings — "Big Boss Man," "Bright Lights, Big City," "Hush, Hush," "Baby What You Want

115

Me To Do" — trying to imitate Reed's hypnotic rhythms on our cheap Silvertone electric guitars, attempting in vain to capture the pain-soaked cries of his mahogany voice in our too-tight, too-white, suburban throats.

However, in placing the phonograph needle again and again in the grooves of Jimmy Reed's records, we began to notice something curious. If one listened very carefully, there could sometimes be heard, ever so faintly in the background, a soft woman's voice murmuring in advance the next verse of the song. The story that grew up around this — and perhaps it is true — was that Jimmy Reed was so absorbed in the bluesy beat and the throbbing guitar riffs of his music that he simply could not remember the words of his own songs. He needed help with the lyrics, and the woman's voice was none other than that of his wife, devotedly coaching her husband through the recording session by whispering the upcoming stanzas into his ear as he sang.

Whether or not this story is accurate, Christians will surely recognize a parallel experience. Jesus tells his followers that the role of the Holy Spirit is, in effect, to whisper the lyrics of the gospel song in the ears of the faithful. When Jesus was present, he was the one who instilled in them the right words, coached them through the proper verses, taught them the joyful commandments. But now that Jesus approaches his death, now that he draws near to his time of departure, now that the disciples will be on their own without him, that task is to be handed over to the Holy Spirit: "If you love me, you will keep my commandments. And I will ask the Father, and he will give you another Advocate, to be with you forever. This is the Spirit of truth . . ." (John 14:15-17).

The primary task, then, of the Holy Spirit is reminding the faithful of the truth, jogging the memories of the followers of Jesus about all of his commandments so that they can keep them in love, whispering the lyrics of the never-ending hymn of faithful obedience in their ears. It may surprise us to think of the Holy Spirit in this way, as a quiet, whispering teacher of the commandments of Jesus. Often the Spirit is advertised in flashier terms: The Spirit gives ecstasy; the Spirit evokes speaking in unknown tongues; the Spirit prompts dramatic and miraculous healings. Indeed, the Holy Spirit of God does perform such deeds, but these are all derivative of the one, primary activity of the Spirit — reminding the children of God about everything that Jesus taught and commanded (John 14:26), whispering the gospel lyrics into the ears of the forgetful faithful.

When Jimmy Carter was running for President of the United States, one of the more vivid moments in the campaign passed by almost unnoticed. One Sunday morning, candidate Carter had been worshipping at the Baptist Church in Plains, Georgia. When the service was over, he exited the church into the swarm of press encamped on the church's front lawn. Cameras whirring, video lights glaring, microphones thrust forward, the media mavens moved in for interviews, pushing themselves to think of clever questions to ask a presidential candidate on the way out of a Southern Baptist Church — "Did you like the sermon?" "Did you enjoy the choir this morning?" "Do you plan to remain a Baptist in Washington?" — on and on the banal questions spewed.

Suddenly, a reporter, probably in a stroke of luck, shouted out a question that genuinely mattered: "Mr. Carter, suppose when you are President, you get into a situation where the laws of the United States are in conflict with what you understand to be the will of God. Which will you follow, the laws of the state or the commandments of God?"

Carter stopped, looked up, and blinked into the bright Georgia sun, obviously turning the question over in his mind. Then, perhaps still "in the Spirit on the Lord's Day," perhaps with the Spirit gently whispering the lyrics of the gospel into his ears, he turned toward the reporter and replied, "I would obey the commandments of God." Alert aides, alarmed by this candor, unnerved by their candidate's near-treasonous remark, hurriedly whisked him away from the press and into a waiting car. Carter the politician should have avoided the question, or hewed closely to the law of the land, but Carter the Christian had the Holy Spirit of Jesus Christ whispering in his ear, "Do you love me? The world cannot see or know me, but do you love me? Do you keep my commandments?"

The reason we need the Holy Spirit murmuring the gospel in our ears, of course, is that we are notoriously forgetful. As one commentator has pointed out, "an early Christian definition for being lost . . . was 'to have amnesia.' "[1] We are amnesiacs who cannot keep our calling clearly in mind. Like the great Jimmy Reed, we are caught up in the rhythms, but we forget the lyrics. We know that we are created to serve and love one another, but the pressure builds and the temptation to seek revenge is strong and we simply forget who we are and what we are purposed to do and be in life.

The doctrine of sin discloses that our loss of memory is not a momentary lapse. Having lost our memory, we now choose forgetfulness again and again, preferring the oblivion of amnesia to the sharp accountability of remembering the commandments. In his book *Lost In The Cosmos: The Last Self-Help Book,* Walker Percy describes a frequent device of soap operas, movies and novels. A principal character will develop amnesia. He or she is in a new place, with a new job, a new set of friends, perhaps a new lover. This plot device, says Percy, is endlessly fascinating since it feeds our fantasies about a risk-free forgetting of the old self and the embarking on a new identity.

Percy decides to push the question of amnesia to its highest power. "Imagine," he writes, "a soap opera in which a character awakens every morning with amnesia . . . ." Every day, the character is in a strange house with a strange and attractive man or woman. Everything is new and fresh — the view from the window, the partner, the sense of the self. "Does this prospect intrigue you?" asks Percy. "If it does, what does this say about your non-amnesiac self?"[2]

Percy's point, of course, is the lure of forgetfulness. One way to describe sin is willful forgetfulness. We choose amnesia; we decide as an act of the will not to remember that we are God's very own son, God's very own daughter.

God's mercy is, in part, the grace of memory. God's Spirit whispers in our ear, telling us what we cannot — or will not — remember, refreshing our memory about who we are and to whom we belong. When, in situations of challenge and stress, we remember the comfort and demand of the gospel, it is because the voice of the Holy Spirit whispers the lyrics in our ear.

A friend who is a minister reported her experience in taking communion to a woman in a nursing home who had Alzheimer's disease. When she arrived in the woman's room, she attempted to carry on a conversation with her. Even though she was a member of this minister's church and the minister had known her for years, meaningful communication was nearly impossible. The woman was confused and disoriented. She simply could not remember anything, including who she was or who the minister was.

When the minister set up the communion elements, the woman's confusion increased. Seeing the bread and the cup on her hospital table, she furrowed her brow and tried to sweep them off with her hand, "What's this? What . . .?"

But when the minister began the familiar communion liturgy, the woman grew calm. The Holy Spirit irrigated furrows in her memory deeper than any disease, more profound than any confusion. "On the night that our Lord was betrayed . . .," the minister said, and the woman began to repeat the words silently with her lips. "This is my body, for you," the woman was now quietly speaking the words along with the minister, the Spirit whispering the lyrics in her ear. When the bread and the wine were offered, the woman eagerly, hungrily, took them in her hands — the gifts of God for this daughter of God.[3]

In his book *The Man Who Mistook His Wife For A Hat,* Oliver Sacks tells the story of Jimmie, a former sailor, now a patient in a nursing home, whose severe neurological disorder had left him with a profound and permanent amnesia. He simply had no memory of anything from 1945 on. Having no ability to retrieve the past and no ability to construct a meaningful present, Jimmie lacked the continuity that makes for a sense of the self. He was, wrote Sacks, a person who "wore a look of infinite sadness and resignation."

However, when Sacks asked the Sisters who ran the nursing home whether Jimmie had lost his soul, the Sisters were outraged by the question. "Watch Jimmie in chapel," they said, "and judge for yourself."

So Sacks did watch Jimmie in chapel, and there he observed an astounding transformation. He saw an intensity and steadiness in Jimmie that he had not observed before. As he received the sacrament, there was "perfect alignment of his spirit with the spirit of the Mass." There in worship, Jimmie was no longer at the mercy of a faulty and fallible memory. "He was wholly held, absorbed . . . ." He whose mind was broken was given in worship, "a continuity and unity so seamless it could not permit any break."[4]

Jimmie in his own way is like all of us. In the final analysis, none of us is able to construct a self. We must all be given a story and a continuity not of our own making. Where we have no faithful memory, God remembers, and by the grace of God, the Spirit whispers the lyrics of the saving gospel in our ears.

---

1. Fred B. Craddock, *John* (Atlanta: John Knox Press, 1982), p. 113.

2. Walker, Percy, *Lost In The Cosmos: The Last Self-Help Book* (New York: Farrar, Strauss, and Giroux, 1983), pp. 17-19.

3. I am grateful to the Rev. Joanna Adams of Atlanta, Georgia, for this story.

4. The story, from Oliver Sacks, *The Man Who Mistook His Wife For A Hat,* is reported in Craig Dykstra, "Memory and Truth," *Theology Today*, XLIV/2, p. 162.

Easter 7
John 17:1-11

Praying To The Congregation

According to legend, a certain West Coast radio evangelist would customarily close his broadcasts by praying over the air, "O God, we ask that today you would touch the hearts of those in 'Radioland' to support this worldwide ministry. We pray that you would move them mightily to send offerings of love, and to send them to Post Office Box 345, Pasadena, California."

Though he was particularly crass about it, this minister was actually committing a fairly common mistake in worship leadership — praying to the congregation. This liturgical *faux pas* occurs whenever a worship leader loses sight of the fact that the true audience of prayer is God and not the congregation overhearing and joining in the prayer. Prayers may be poetic, but they are not poetry recitals for an audience; they may be sung or danced, but they are not performances for the crowd; they may be filled with the grit and anguish of the world, but they are not addressed *to* the world. Prayer is communication to and with God. Prayers are properly spoken to God, and God alone.

This seems obvious, of course, but many worship leaders periodically lose their grip on this truth with the unfortunate result that congregations, bowing their heads reverently to participate in prayer, suddenly discover that they are really the targets of it. "Lord," intones the minister, "We pray today that those present would know, indeed would truly know in their souls, that . . .," followed by a didactic reprise of the three points of the just-preached sermon. Or, perhaps, the prayer leader will solemnly state, "God, in a troubled time such as our age, many have fallen into the woeful habit of . . .," usually followed by a stern scold of the congregation for poor worship attendance, stingy giving, lax parental discipline, or whatever else seems to be peeving the minister these days.

Not long ago in a seminary chapel service, the worship leader prayed, "O God our comfort, heal the wounds of those suffering in war-torn Bosnia, formerly Yugoslavia." To be sure, the maps in the back of the Bible are out of date. Even so, God probably did not need the geography lesson. The truth be known, this worship leader was no doubt fearful that those overhearing this prayer, behind on the news, would have missed the renaming of Yugoslavia, thus, we are given yet another example of the classic liturgical error — praying to the congregation.

Praying to the congregation is a liturgical violation all right, but before we give students a failing grade in worship for this transgression, we need to deal with the fact that Jesus himself seems to be a repeat offender. Especially in the Gospel of John, Jesus' prayers to God sound suspiciously like sermons to his disciples. In fact, on one occasion, the author of John makes the comment that a certain prayer of Jesus was intended as a teaching device. In other words, Jesus, it seems, *intentionally* prayed to the congregation (John 12:32-33).

Indeed, on another occasion, Jesus himself actually confesses to the crime. Looking heavenward, Jesus prays (presumably in a loud voice), "Father, I thank you for having heard me." Then, he adds under his breath, "I knew that you always hear me, but I have said this for the sake of the crowd standing here, so that they may believe that you sent me" (John 11:41-42). Prayer words spoken "for the sake of the crowd"? This is a clear-cut case of praying to the congregation.

But before we pull Jesus over and ticket him for a liturgical infraction, we need to make two key observations. First, when Jesus prays to the congregation, he is following in a long biblical tradition. Many of the psalms, for example, move fluidly back and forth between pleas to God and appeals to fellow worshippers. Moses, when he prayed his great prayer to the heavens (Deuteronomy 32-33), could not seem to keep it quite straight whether he was speaking to God or speaking to Israel. Or again, Paul, in some of his letters, moves like a weaver's shuttle between doxology and discourse, between prayer and persuasion. Jesus' prayers stand, then, among the great company of biblical prayers, for the Bible itself seems to blur the line between praying to God and praying to the congregation.[1]

The second observation we need to make is to note a crucial distinction between two different types of praying to the congregation. Most praying to the congregation — the adverse kind — occurs when the one praying forgets about God, loses sight of the true character of prayer, and merely uses prayer language to mask a teachy lecture, a commercial for a church program, or a self-serving emotional pitch.

The second type, the kind that we find in the Bible and in the prayer life of Jesus, is altogether different. Here, the one praying never loses sight of God, never breaks free of the primary bond with God, and is, therefore, always aware that prayer takes place in the context of communion with God. Indeed, it is precisely because prayer is communion — human beings in intimate relationship with God — that the language of prayer takes the form of a conversation, communication moving in two directions at the same time.

Because prayer occurs in relationship to God, it is a profound expression of ourselves and our needs to God, but it is also a profound revelation of God to us. In prayer, we say things we need to say, but we also see and know things —

about God and about ourselves — that we could not see or know apart from the illumination of the Spirit in the intimacy of prayer's communion.

Take, for example, the phrase from the Lord's Prayer, "Give us this day our daily bread." This is, to be sure, a petition addressed to God; we are speaking these words *to* God, asking for something *from* God. But as we speak these words to God, God also speaks through them to us. As we say to God "Give us this day our daily bread," the Spirit enables the tide of communication to flow in the other direction, too, guiding our imaginations into the everyday world of bread and nourishment. We cannot pray these words over and over again without imagining the rich grain slowly growing in the field, the heavy turning of the millstone grinding out the flour, the hands that deftly knead the dough, the loaves rising in the warm oven, the joy of table fellowship and, most of all, the hidden hand of Providence that bestows all of these things as good gifts. As we pray in the Spirit, then, we are being taught by the Spirit. As we reach out to God, God reaches out to us, and undergirding all prayer is communion with God.

It is precisely this communion, this intimacy, with God that is the theme of Jesus' prayer in today's text. John 17 is very clearly a prayer to God — Jesus looks up at heaven and addresses his words to God — but it is also a stunning example of the best kind of praying to the congregation. Every word of Jesus' prayer flows toward God, and, likewise, every word is intended to be overheard by the church and is expressly aimed at teaching the faithful. What it teaches is that Jesus Christ has made it possible for us, too, to be in intimate relationship with God. Because the obedient Son remained in faithful and unbroken communion with the Father, those who belong to the Son may share this closeness. "And this is eternal life, that they may know you, the only true God .... All mine are yours, and yours are mine; and I have been glorified in them" (John 17:3, 10).

In this regard, this prayer, like the Lord's Prayer, is a model prayer — a prayer about prayer. All prayers, whether they

124

are prayers pleading for a season of world peace or prayers begging for a moment of inner peace, are really prayers yearning for God to embrace us. We pray for food and health and justice and forgiveness and protection — and truly these are our needs — but beneath it all we are really praying for God to be with us, for God to hold us close, for God never to forget us or to abandon us to ourselves. Therefore, however much we may speak of our prayers being answered, the truth is that prayers are the answer since, in our praying, we are given what we most deeply need — communion with God.

In her book, *The Preaching Life,* Episcopal priest Barbara Brown Taylor tells of her experience, early in her ministry, planning adult education for a local church. Whenever she would poll the adults in the congregation about what sort of educational experiences they would prefer, the answer would always come back the same: they wanted Bible study. So, taking this at face value, Taylor would arrange for Bible studies of the finest sort. She would contract with professors at a nearby theological seminary to come and teach serious Bible classes. She would publicize these classes widely. However, people stayed away in droves.

Finally, it dawned on her that, when people asked for Bible study, what they really wanted was not information about the Bible; what they wanted was an experience of God. Asking for Bible study was the only way they knew to ask for what they really wanted — intimacy with God. So, she began a different kind of Bible study, one that turned out to be much more successful. She writes:

> *I laid off the seminary professors and offered a class on biblical meditation instead. The plan was simple: every week we locked the door, took off our shoes, closed our eyes and listened to a [Bible] story ... We shot down reality in front of our eyes. We hung "Gone fishin' " signs on our eyelids and let our imaginations take us places we had never been.* [2]

The places they had never been, of course, the places they wanted desperately to go, were the places where God was. It was intimacy with God they sought — that we seek.

In a scene from *Shadowlands*, a film based on the life of C.S. Lewis, Lewis has returned to Oxford from London, where he has just been married to Joy Gresham, an American woman, in a private Episcopal ceremony performed at her hospital bedside. She is dying from cancer, and, through the struggle with her illness, she and Lewis have been discovering the depth of their love for each other. As Lewis arrives at the college where he teaches, he is met by Harry Harrington, an Episcopal priest, who asks what news there is. Lewis hesitates; then, deciding to speak of the marriage and not the cancer, he says, "Ah, good news, I think, Harry. Yes, good news."

Harrington, not aware of the marriage and thinking that Lewis is referring to Joy's medical situation, replies, "I know how hard you've been praying .... Now, God is answering your prayer."

"That's not why I pray, Harry," Lewis responds. "I pray because I can't help myself. I pray because I'm helpless. I pray because the need flows out of me all the time, waking and sleeping. It doesn't change God; it changes *me*."[3]

It doesn't change God; it changes *me*. Prayer is not a message scribbled on a note, jammed into a bottle and tossed into the sea in hopes that it will wash up someday on God's shoreline. Prayer is communion with God. We speak to God, but God touches, embraces, shapes and changes us. Whether we pray for rain or pray for sunshine, our prayer is answered, because in the act of praying we receive the gift we really seek — intimacy with God.

---

1. The discussion of the biblical examples of mixing prayers to God with addresses to the hearers is informed by Fred B. Craddock, *John* (Atlanta: John Knox Press, 1982), p. 122.

2. Barbara Brown Taylor, *The Preaching Life* (Cambridge and Boston: Cowley Publications, 1993), p. 47.

3. From the movie *Shadowlands*, copyright 1993, Savoy Pictures, Inc.

Ascension Of The Lord
Luke 24:44-53 (C, L)
Matthew 28:16-20 (RC)

Country Songs And Easter Hymns

As the van rolled down the interstate, Kitty Wells' hillbilly alto rattled the radio speakers; "When you're lookin' at me," she belted out, "you're lookin' at country." In the van were ten of us, all seminary seniors, heading away from our rural South Carolina campus toward the big city of Atlanta, and Kitty Wells had it right: If you were looking at us, you were looking at country.

It was not that we urbanly-challenged folk actually wanted to go to the city; the faculty was forcing us to do so. Terrified that our education in the outlands was forming us into unsophisticated rustics, our professors wanted us to spend a month in the city, grabbing the high-tension wires of urban life. So, we were uprooted from the comforts of home and land and family, dislodged from the pleasures of long, lazy, bucolic afternoons and thrust into the noise and strife of a million strangers where we were, like it or not, to take a crash course called "Urban Ministry."

It did not take long for our worst fears to be confirmed. "Urban Ministry" turned out to be a continuous stream of being shouted at by shopkeepers, rudely scurried off the streets by hostile city drivers, and generally hassled by the urban crush. After only a few days of this, we were, frankly, ready to go back to provincial "Galilee," so much so that we petitioned our professors to allow us to go home. The petition was flatly denied. "We brought you to the city for an experience," they replied, "and you're not leaving until you've had it."

Brought to the city for an experience and forbidden to leave until we'd had it. Since that faculty fiat, I have always had great sympathy for the disciples as they are described in the Gospel of Luke. Luke's picture of them is different from the other gospels. In Luke, the emphasis falls upon the disciples' connection to the city. By contrast, in Mark, part of the good news of the resurrection is that the disciples are told to go back home to Galilee. The women discover the empty tomb, and the angel says, "He has been raised. He is not here. Tell his disciples to meet him in Galilee." Matthew is even better. Jesus *himself* appears to the women with the comforting call to return to Galilee, "Do not be afraid. Tell my disciples they will see me in Galilee." In regard to Mark and Matthew, as Kitty Wells would have put it in her tremolo twang, "If you're looking for Jesus, you'll look in the country."

But not Luke. "Stay in the *city*," says the risen Christ, "until you are clothed with power." It is clear that, in Luke, the disciples are not going to be allowed the rural pleasures, but are in for a course in "Urban Ministry." Jesus, who "set his face to go to Jerusalem," now tells his disciples "I brought you to this city for an experience, and you're not leaving until you've had it.

Now, New Testament scholars have made it clear that we are not just talking about geography here, but also theology. For Matthew and Mark, Galilee is, well, the actual Galilee, but a metaphor for something more as well: the place of beginnings. And for Luke, the city is the real city, the Jerusalem of streets and smells and strangers, but it is also a theological symbol.

For Luke, the city is the place the earliest church waited for Pentecost or, to put it more dynamically, it is the place where the church always waits for the Spirit. For Luke, the city is not initially a place where the church flexes its muscle and performs ministry, it is first and foremost the place where the church waits *without* power to receive its ministry, or, rather, to receive what it cannot produce on its own: the strength and ability to do ministry in the first place. Jesus was tempted in the wilderness, in the bleak and lonely countryside, at the "end of the earth" so to speak, and then, in the power of the Spirit he entered the city to perform his great work of redemption. Now the church, in his name, must be tested in the city, so that in the power of the Spirit, it may continue Jesus' work of redemption to the ends of the earth.

For Luke, the city is, of course, Jerusalem, but it is also every place where Christians keep their eyes open to learn the ways of God in the world, where they discern their identity before asserting it, where they experience the world God loves before trying to transform it, where they learn that God does not empower the church before it is ready for power, God's power. The city is the place where disciples must prepare for the cause of Christ before championing it. The city is not just Jerusalem but Chicago and Atlanta, Middletown and Moscow, Seoul and Sandusky, Nairobi and New York. As a symbol, the "city" can be any place, but Luke knew that it sometimes happens best in the real city.

What is it that the church can see and experience as it waits in the city? For one thing, the church can learn how to pray for justice. In Luke, and only in Luke, Jesus once told his disciples an urban story that turned out to be a lesson about the power of prayer (Luke 18:1-8). According to the story, there was in the city a judge who neither feared God nor respected humanity. He didn't go to church, and he refused to give to the United Way. But there was also a widow in this city who kept knocking on his chamber door and demanding justice. The judge could not care less. Despite the widow's constant lament, he refused to budge, kept the door locked, said he didn't need her vote. But she continued to demand justice until, finally, exhausted by her ceaseless appeal, the judge slapped his forehead and cried, "I'm not a religious man and I'm not a humanitarian either, but this woman is wearing me out. I've got to give her some justice."

Now that is definitely a city story, full of the clamor and conflict of the metropolis. In fact, the meditative monk Thomas Merton would probably have said that this is a typical city story involving recognizable city types like a godless judge and a strident and noisy citizen. The city, according to Merton, was a dramatic symbol of the world without God. Its "ceaseless motion of . . . angry people in a . . . swirl of frustration," he thought, prevents people from contemplating and, by nature, cuts them off from any real relation to God.[1]

To this, the Jesus of the Gospel of Luke would have responded, "I love you Thomas Merton, but you listen to that city story and you will discover much about prayer. If you really want to learn to pray you need to listen not only to the meditations in the monastery and the language of quiet contemplation but also to the noisy cries for justice in the city streets. God grants justice to those who noisily cry out day and night."

It is no mistake, then, that Jesus told a city story to make a point about prayer. If one listens to the rhythms and cries of the city, beneath the cacophony one can hear prayer, for at the base of every authentic prayer is a plea for justice — a hunger for God to set things right. Not only that, but Jesus also knew that capacity of even the godless city to supply, here and there, moments of justice, like a widow's plea finally heard by a begrudging judge, is a sign of answered prayer, a sign of God's Spirit moving in the world to set things right.

No wonder the disciples are told, "Stay in the city until you receive power." If they keep their eyes open, they will learn about prayer and justice.

One cool September night at Yankee Stadium in New York, a foul ball was hit into the lower left field stands. It was heading right toward a boy of about nine who had obviously come to the game that night hoping for just such a moment. He

132

had a pair of cheap binoculars around his neck and was wearing an oversized Yankees cap and a small Little League glove which had the hardly-broken-in look of a mitt worn by a kid you let play right field in the late innings of hopeless games. The foul ball was arching directly toward this boy's outstretched hand, but suddenly, a man of about 35 wearing an expensive knit shirt and horn-rimmed glasses reached over the boy, jostling him aside, and caught the ball. In the jostle, the plastic binoculars were broken, and the boy, despite his mother's comfort, was clearly crushed. Everybody in the left field stands had seen this, and, after a second or two of stunned silence, someone shouted, "Give the kid the ball!" Then another cried, "Give the kid the ball!" A couple of rows joined in unison, "Give the kid the ball!"

Horn Rims shook his head and put the ball in his pocket. That inflamed the whole left field crowd, and with one voice they took up the chant, "Give the kid the ball!" It spread to the center field stands, then to right field, until the whole outfield, including people who did not even know the story, were shouting, "Give the kid the ball!" Players began to glance up from the field to the stands to see what was going on.

Horn Rims remained stubbornly firm. Finally, a man got up out of his seat, walked over to Horn Rims and spoke some words patiently and gently to him. Horn Rims hesitated, then reached into his pocket and handed the ball to the kid. "He *gave* the kid the ball!" someone exclaimed. Then the whole stands thundered, "He gave the kid the ball!" Applause rippled around the stadium.

Then an even more strange thing began to happen. When another foul ball landed in the left field stands, the man who caught it walked over to Horn Rims and gave it to him. Horn Rims, incredulously, thanked him and took it. The next foul ball was caught by a man in a muscle shirt who was sporting a Fu Manchu mustache. He turned and tossed the ball to the kid, who, to everyone's delight and surprise, caught it. More enthusiastic applause from the crowd, who had come that night to see a baseball game but witnessed instead a city parable about justice and grace.[2] Stay in the city until you receive power.

The city is a parable not only for prayer; it is also a parable of human community. It is in the city that we learn best that everyone is not just like we are. Indeed, it was in the city that the disciples learned that the community of Jesus Christ is broader than we have imagined. It was in a city called Nain that they learned that the kingdom embraced widows and prostitutes. The man whose name was "Legion" was from a city, and Luke and Matthew both tell the Parable of the Great Banquet, where those who were invited made excuses, and so the host sent the servants out to bring in enough guests for the banquet. Only in Luke, though, are we specifically told that this is a city story about urban people: "Go out into the streets and lanes of the city and bring in the poor and the maimed, the blind and the lame" (Luke 14:15-24).

Parker Palmer has remarked that the church speaks often about "community," but it is often an idealized community. We talk about the "church family" or *kononia* groups, but what we really mean to describe is a group of people just like us. Such images of community are, thus, idolatrous. That is why the real city — not the make-believe city — is the place where the church can best learn about the kingdom community. Palmer offers this definition of community: "Community is that place where the person you least want to live with always lives. And when that person moves away, someone else arises to take his or her place."[3]

In this sense, then, every place where the church is planted is, in its own way, a "city." There is no village so small, no place so isolated, that there is not at least some taste of the richness, the challenge, and, quite frankly, the grating difficulty, of human differences. It is there in the wild diversity of the "city" — wherever it may be found — that the church gains true power, the power that is like Jesus' power, the power that does not protect itself from the stranger, does not seize things from the neighbor, but which lives for the neighbor and welcomes the stranger.

134

There is a neighborhood grocery store in our fairly affluent town that is visited each morning by the same clearly non-affluent person. We will call her "Ruth," and she is a street person. She enters the grocery about 11 a.m. every day and makes her way through the aisles. There is no polite way to describe what she does: Ruth steals food. Each morning she gathers enough for her lunch, poking pieces of fruit, loaves of bread, wedges of cheese, or a can of meat under her torn and stained coat. She then glides out the door. But she is not very subtle about it. Everyone at the store can see what she does. The stockroom crew know she is taking food; the butcher sees her activity; the checkout clerks are aware of her pilfering; the manager knows what she is about.

Not long ago, this grocery moved several blocks away to a larger building. The week they moved to the new location, the store manager telephoned a downtown pastor. "I don't want to embarrass Ruth," he began, "so would you please find her and tell her where we've moved. I want to be sure she can find us."

There in the city is a parable of mercy. An urban grocery store owner wants to be sure a homeless woman, a woman very much unlike the owner, can nonetheless find food, and for disciples with discerning eyes, there is much to learn here about the power of God in the world. "Stay in the city with your eyes open to the grace of God," the disciples are told, "and you will receive power."

So the church waited in the city, and when it was gathered in one place on Pentecost Day, they did indeed receive power. According to the story, Parthians and Medes, Cretans and Arabs, visitors from Rome, street people and welfare mothers, and kids with Little League gloves all heard the gospel in their own language. And with a power they never imagined, the power of the Spirit of God, they walked boldly into the future proclaiming the grace of Jesus Christ.

1. See the discussion of Merton's anti-city views in Harvey Cox, *The Seduction Of The Spirit* (New York: Simon and Schuster, 1973), p. 68.

2. "Metropolitan Diary," *The New York Times,* June 20, 1984.

3. Parker J. Palmer, *The Company Of Strangers* (New York: Crossroad, 1981), pp. 124-125.